D0041858

A Commonplace Book

★

ALEC GUINNESS

A Commonplace Book

HAMISH HAMILTON
an imprint of
PENGUIN BOOKS

HAMISH HAMILTON

Published by the Penguin Group
Penguin Books Ltd, 80 Strand, London WC2R 0RL, England
Penguin Putnam Inc., 375 Hudson Street, New York, New York 10014, USA
Penguin Books Australia Ltd, Ringwood, Victoria, Australia
Penguin Books Canada Ltd, 10 Alcorn Avenue, Toronto, Ontario, Canada M4V 3B2
Penguin Books India (P) Ltd, 11 Community Centre,
Panchsheel Park, New Delhi – 110 017, India
Penguin Books (NZ) Ltd, Cnr Rosedale and Airborne Roads,
Albany, Auckland, New Zealand
Penguin Books (South Africa) (Pty) Ltd, 24 Sturdee Avenue, Rosebank 2196, South Africa

Penguin Books Ltd, Registered Offices: 80 Strand, London WC2R 0RL, England

www.penguin.com

First published 2001
1

Set in 12.25/15pt Monotype Fournier
Typeset by Rowland Phototypesetting Ltd, Bury St Edmunds, Suffolk
Printed in Great Britain by Clays Ltd, St Ives plc

A CIP catalogue record for this book is available from the British Library

ISBN 0–241–14146–X

Publisher's Note

Sir Alec Guinness died in August 2000, at the age of eighty-six. His last book, an extended journal entitled *A Positively Final Appearance*, was published by Hamish Hamilton in 1999 and in paperback by Penguin a year later. At his death he left behind two lined exercise books, as described in his Introduction, filled with handwritten entries, which together make up something between a commonplace book and a journal. In addition, he had begun to type up some of the entries, and had written the Introduction, which strongly suggests that he had publication or performance in mind. It is known that he was planning to record some of the items on an audio tape to be circulated to a small number of friends after his death, but died before this could be done.

A number of brief entries in note form have been omitted from *A Commonplace Book*, but nothing has been added; and, rather than attempt to group the entries by themes, it has been decided to keep the order in which they appear in the exercise books. The illustrations were commissioned by the publisher.

Introduction

For as far back as I can remember I have been attracted
by lovely, white sheets of virgin paper. As a child I
quickly and enthusiastically defaced these with elaborate
drawings of fierce naval battles. Later on I took to
buying, when funds allowed, rather nice-looking large
notebooks into which I copied, in my best italic script,
poems I intended to learn – but rarely did – or pieces of
prose that pleased me. I doubt if I ever filled more than
ten pages of any of these commonplace books before a
new and more handsome one caught my eye; and I would
start all over again. Almost all of them have been lost,
abandoned or destroyed. But a few years ago I struck out
on a slightly different line; instead of attractive, expensive
books of blank paper (and some of the modern Italian
ones are very tempting) I took to buying the cheapest
school exercise books, feint-ruled, and scribbling in my
now nearly illegible hand the odds and ends that have
caught my eye – much of it, I expect, familiar to you –
and it is from these exercise books that I have culled these
pages. There is no theme or shape to all this, but now and
then I have placed a few things side by side, as the con-
trast or similarity amused me, and I have interjected a few
one-liners – just for the hell of it.

Alec Guinness

Like many of us, I have often wondered about the sources of Shakespeare's imagination — whether it sprang from his conscious memory, or from something once heard or seen and apparently half forgotten. Here are a couple of brief examples:

'Come unto these yellow sands,
    And then take hands;
Curtsied when you have, and kiss'd
    The wild waves whist.'
      William Shakespeare, *The Tempest*

'Far from the town (when all is whist and still,
Save that the sea, playing on yellow sand,
Sends forth a rattling murmur to the land,
Whose sound allures the golden Morpheus
In silence of the night to visit us).'
      Christopher Marlowe, *Hero and Leander*

Florio's translation of Montaigne was published in England in 1603. Shakespeare registered Hamlet *in 1603, although there had been a performance in 1602.*

From Florio's translation of Montaigne:
'A wisdom . . . so precisely circumspect is the enemy of doing.'

And from Hamlet:
           '. . . Now, whether it be
Bestial oblivion, or some craven scruple
Of thinking too precisely on the event
(A thought which, quarter'd, hath but one part wisdom
And ever three parts coward) I do not know
Why yet I live to say, "This thing's to do" . . .'

    ✻

'This horrible duality has often given me matter for reflection. Oh, this terrible second me, always seated whilst the other is on foot, acting, living, suffering, bestirring itself. This second me that I have never been able to intoxicate, to make shed tears, or put to sleep. And how it sees into things, and how it mocks.'

    Alphonse Daudet, *Notes on Life*

    ✻

I hope I have got my facts right about this. Last week the National Gallery put back on its walls the glorious Wilton Diptych, created about 600 years ago and showing Richard II kneeling, clothed in shimmering gold. It has recently been cleaned and a small but extraordinary detail has been revealed. (I have not yet had the opportunity to see it.) On the top of a banner in the painting is a tiny circle, about a centimetre in diameter. For ages this has been seen as a dark, tarnished blank. The cleaning shows it to be a minute painting of an island, with tropical trees and a castle surrounded by a silver sea. The Diptych *once belonged to Charles I but its history before that is vague. I suppose it is* just *possible that Shakespeare once saw it, or at any rate heard someone describe it. John of Gaunt, in* Richard II, *has:*

'This royal throne of kings, this scepter'd isle,
This earth of majesty, this seat of Mars,
This other Eden, demi-paradise . . .'

And:
'This precious stone set in the silver sea.'

✳

Shakespeare's Dogs

The names of Shakespeare's dogs are: Mocker, Mountain, Silver, Fury, Tyrant, Tray, Blanche, Sweetheart. And, in The Two Gentlemen of Verona, *Launce's shameless dog —* Crab.

Crab! Crab! 'I think Crab my dog be the sourest-natured dog that lives . . . He is a stone, a very pebble stone.'

'One that I brought up of a puppy; one that I saved from drowning, when three or four of his blind brothers and sisters went to it . . . I was sent to deliver him as a present to Mistress Silvia from my master; and I came no sooner

into the dining chamber but he steps me to her trencher
and steals her capon's leg. O, 'tis a foul thing when a cur
cannot keep himself in all companies . . . If I had not had
more wit than he, to take a fault upon me that he did, I
think verily he had been hanged for't; sure as I live, he
had suffered for't; you shall judge. He thrusts me himself
into the company of three or four gentleman-like dogs
under the duke's table; he has not been there – bless the
mark – a pissing while, but all the chamber smelt him.
"Out with the dog!" says one. "What cur is that?" says
another. "Whip him out," says a third. "Hang him up,"
says the duke. I, having been acquainted with the smell
before, knew it was Crab, and goes to the fellow that
whips the dogs. "Friend," quoth I, "you mean to whip

the dog?" "Ay, marry do I," quoth he. "You do him the more wrong," quoth I, "'twas I did the thing you wot of." He makes no more ado but whips me out of the chamber. How many masters would do this for his servant? Nay, I'll be sworn, I have sat in the stocks for puddings he hath stolen, otherwise he had been executed; I have stood on the pillory for geese he hath killed, otherwise he had suffered for't. Thou thinkest not of this now. Nay, I remember the trick you served me when I took my leave of Madam Silvia; did not I bid thee still mark me and do as I do? When didst thou see me heave up my leg and make water against a gentlewoman's farthingale? Didst thou ever see me do such a trick?'

Crab! Crab!

✳

'If ever the last 50,000 years of man's existence were divided into lifetimes of approximately sixty-two years each, there have been about 800 lifetimes. Of these 800 at least 650 were spent in caves. Only during the last seventy lifetimes has it been possible to communicate effectively from one lifetime to another – as writing made it possible to do. Only during the last six lifetimes did masses of men ever see the printed word. Only during the last four has it been possible to measure time with any precision. Only in the last two has anyone used an electric motor. And the overwhelming majority of all material goods we use in daily life today have been developed within the present 800th lifetime.'

Hans Küng, *On Being a Christian*

Of the writer Clemence Dane (Winifred Ashton) J. B. Priestley said:

'As for Clemence Dane, she takes a pre-Caxton view of books, and the sight of print on the page excites her to madness.'

At a small luncheon party given by Priestley he told a slightly scurrilous story about a lady known to all present. When he had finished, Mrs Priestley reprimanded him, saying, 'Jack, that is not strictly true.' To which he replied, 'Never mind; it's good enough for general conversation.'

We and They

Father, Mother, and Me,
   Sister and Auntie say
All the people like us are We,
   And every one else is They.
And They live over the sea,
   While We live over the way,
But would you believe it? — They look upon We
   As only a sort of They!

We eat pork and beef
   With cow-horn-handled knives.
They who gobble Their rice off a leaf
   Are horrified out of Their lives;
While They who live up a tree,
   And feast on grubs and clay,
(Isn't it scandalous?) look upon We
   As a simply disgusting They!

We shoot birds with a gun.
   They stick lions with spears.
Their full-dress is un-.
   We dress up to Our ears.
They like Their friends for tea.
   We like Our friends to stay;
And, after all that, They look upon We
   As an utterly ignorant They!

We eat kitcheny food.
   We have doors that latch.
They drink milk or blood,
   Under an open thatch.
We have Doctors to fee.
   They have Wizards to pay.
And (impudent heathen!) They look upon We
   As a quite impossible They!

All good people agree,
   And all good people say,
All nice people, like Us, are We,
   And every one else is They:
But if you cross over the sea,
   Instead of over the way,
You may end by (think of it!) looking on We
   As only a sort of They!

    Rudyard Kipling

   ✳

'As I sat at the café, I said to myself,
They may talk as they please about what they call pelf,
They may sneer as they like about eating and drinking,
But help it I cannot, I cannot help thinking
   How pleasant it is to have money, heigh ho!
   How pleasant it is to have money.

I sit at my table *en grand seigneur*,
And when I have done, throw a crust to the poor;

Not only the pleasure, one's self, of good living,
But also the pleasure of now and then giving.
 So pleasant it is to have money, heigh ho!
 So pleasant it is to have money . . .

I drive through the streets, and I care not a damn;
The people they stare, and they ask who I am;
And if I should chance to run over a cad,
I can pay for the damage if ever so bad.

So pleasant it is to have money, heigh ho!
So pleasant it is to have money.

We stroll to our box and look down on the pit,
And if it weren't low should be tempted to spit;
We loll and we talk until people look up,
And when it's half over we go out and sup.
  So pleasant it is to have money, heigh ho!
  So pleasant it is to have money . . .

They may talk as they please about what they call pelf,
And how one ought never to think of one's self,
And how pleasures of thought surpass eating and
      drinking –
My pleasure of thought is the pleasure of thinking
  How pleasant it is to have money, heigh ho!
  How pleasant it is to have money.'

   Arthur Hugh Clough, *Spectator ab Extra*

        ✳

'E. F. Benson never lived his life at all; only stayed with it
and lunched with it.'
   A. C. Benson

        ✳

LORD FOPPINGTON: 'Well, 'tis an unspeakable pleasure
   to be a man of quality – strike me dumb!'
   Richard Sheridan, *A Trip to Scarborough*

The Reverend William Barnes (1801–1886)

W. H. Auden, in his introduction to Nineteenth-Century Minor Poets, *wrote this:*
'I cannot enjoy one poem by Shelley and am delighted by every line of William Barnes, but I know perfectly well that Shelley is a major poet, and Barnes a minor one.'

Barnes himself wrote of his own work thus:
'Speech was shapen of the breath-sounds of speakers, for the ears of hearers, and not from speech tokens (letters) in books . . . and therefore I have shapen my teaching as that of a speech of breath-sounded words, and not of lettered ones.'

Francis Kilvert, in a diary entry for 30 April 1874, states that Barnes had a knowledge of seventeen languages. In fact he had an understanding of sixty; quite something for the son of a small farmer from the Vale of Blackmoor.

Kilvert was taken by the Vicar of Fordington, near Dorchester, to Winterborne Came Rectory where Barnes lived. He wrote:

'We walked together to the Poet's house. It lies a little back from the glaring white high road and stands on a lawn fringed with trees. It is thatched and a thatched verandah runs along its front. As we turned in at the iron gates and went down the gravel path the poet was walking in the verandah. He welcomed us cordially and brought us into his drawing room. He is an old man, over seventy, rather bowed with age, but apparently hale and strong. "Excuse my study gown," he said. He wore a dark grey loose gown girt round the waist with a black cord and tassel, black knee breeches, black silk stockings and gold-buckled shoes.

'I was immediately struck by the beauty and grandeur of his head. It was an Apostolic head, bald and venerable, and the long soft silvery hair flowed on his shoulders and a long white beard fell upon his breast. His face was handsome and striking, keen yet benevolent, the finely pencilled eyebrows still dark and a beautiful benevolent loving look lighted up his fine dark eyes when they rested upon you. Half hermit, half enchanter.

'Frequently stroking his face and his venerable white beard the Poet told me he had composed his poems chiefly in the evening as a relaxation from the day's work when he kept school in Dorchester.'

White and Blue

My love is of comely height and straight,
And comely in all her ways and gait,
She shows in her face the rose's hue,
And her lids on her eyes are white on blue.

When Elemley clubmen walk'd in May,
And folk came in clusters every way,
As soon as the sun dried up the dew,
And clouds in the sky were white on blue,

She came by the down, with tripping walk,
By daisies and shining banks of chalk,
And brooks with the crowfoot flow'rs to strew
The sky-tinted water, white on blue.

She nodded her head as play'd the band;
She tapp'd with her foot as she did stand;
She danc'd in a reel, and wore all new
A skirt with a jacket, white with blue.

I single her out from thin and stout,
From slender and stout I chose her out;
And what, in the evening, could I do,
But give her my breast-knot, white and blue?

William Barnes

'If you press me to say why I loved him, I feel that it can only be expressed by replying: "Because it was him; because it was me." '

> Montaigne

✻

'Something unpleasant is coming when men are anxious to tell the truth.'

> Benjamin Disraeli

✻

'Do not send me your manuscript. Worse than the practice of writing books about living men is the conduct of living men in supervising such books.'

> A. E. Housman, letter to Houston Martin

✻

'In its kind, which for me has no attraction, and in its metre, which for me has no beauty, I think it is a masterpiece.'

> Gerard Manley Hopkins, letter to Robert Bridges

✻

'And so, as to the judgement of society, a just indignation would be felt against a writer who brought forward, wantonly, the weaknesses of a great man, though the whole world knew that they existed. No one is at liberty to speak ill of another without a justifiable reason, even though he knows he is speaking the truth, and the public knows it too.'

Cardinal Newman, *Apologia Pro Vita Sua*

✳

'Let not the Olive boast of her own fatness, nor the Fig-tree of her own sweetnesse, nor the Vine of her own fruitfulnesse, for we were all but Brambles.'

John Donne, from a sermon

✳

'Till now the doubtful dusk reveal'd
   The knolls once more where, couch'd at ease,
   The white kine glimmer'd, and the trees
Laid their dark arms about the field:

And suck'd from out the distant gloom
   A breeze began to tremble o'er
   The large leaves of the sycamore,
And fluctuate all the still perfume,

And gathering freshlier overhead,
   Rock'd the full-foliaged elms, and swung
   The heavy-folded rose, and flung
The lilies to and fro, and said

"The dawn, the dawn," and died away;
  And East and West, without a breath,
  Mixt their dim lights, like life and death,
To broaden into boundless day.'
  Lord Tennyson, *In Memoriam*

✳

  'But when the fields are still,
And the tired men and dogs all gone to rest,
  And only the white sheep are sometimes seen
  Cross and recross the strips of moon-blanch'd green;
  Come, shepherd, and again renew the quest.'
  Matthew Arnold, *The Scholar Gipsy*

✳

'Soon she struggled to a certain hill-top, and saw far
before her the silent inflooding of the day. Out of the east
it welled and whitened; the darkness trembled into light;
and the stars were extinguished like the street lights of a
human city. The whiteness brightened into silver, the
silver warmed into gold, the gold kindled into pure and
living fire; and the face of the east was burned with ele-
mental scarlet. The day drew its first long breath, steady
and chill; and for leagues around the woods sighed and
shivered.'
  R. L. Stevenson, *Prince Otto*

Legend

Snow-blind the meadow; chiming ice
Struck at the wasted water's rim.
An infant in a stable lay.
A child watched for a sight of Him.

'I would have brought spring flowers,' she said.
'But where I wandered none did grow.'
Young Gabriel smiled, opened his hand,
And blossoms pierced the sudden snow.

She plucked the gold, the red, the green,
And with a garland entered in.
'What is your name?' Young Gabriel said.
The maid she answered, 'Magdalene.'

Charles Causley

Love

Love bade me welcome; yet my soul drew back,
      Guilty of dust and sin.
But quick-ey'd Love, observing me grow slack
      From my first entrance in,
Drew nearer to me, sweetly questioning,
      If I lacked anything.

'A guest,' I answer'd, 'worthy to be here';
      Love said, 'You shall be he.'
'I, the unkind, ungrateful? Ah, my dear,
      I cannot look on Thee.'
Love took my hand, and smiling did reply.
      'Who made the eyes but I?'

'Truth, Lord; but I have marr'd them; let my shame
      Go where it doth deserve.'
'And know you not,' says Love, 'Who bore the blame?'
      'My dear, then I will serve.'
'You must sit down,' says Love, 'and taste My meat.'
      So I did sit and eat.

George Herbert

'The incommunicable part of us is the pasture of God.'
Teilhard de Chardin

✸

'Things have come to a pretty pass when religion is allowed to invade the sphere of private life.'
Lord Melbourne

Brief Lives in not so Brief

John Aubrey had a nose for news,
In many a closet did he pry,
And on each side of his nose for news
John Aubrey had an eye for an eie.
See now his note on Francis Bacon,
Who died dishonoured and forsaken:
'He had a delicately, lively, hazel Eie;
Dr Harvey told me it was like the Eie of a viper.'

When Aubrey drank with Edmund Wyld
At the Blackmores Head in Bloomsbury,
The talk inevitably turned
To aspects of the human eie.
The satirist, Sir John Birkenhead,
Whose poems I have never read,
'Was of middling stature, great goggli eies,
Not of sweet aspect.'

John Aubrey was a genial man;
I fancy that as he imbibed
A host of eies rolled through his brain,
All clamouring to be described.
Woulds't know the true philosopher's look?
Pause and consider Robert Hooke:
'His head is large; his eie full and popping,
And not quick; a grey eie.'

He garnered eies in town and shire
And on the winding roads between 'em,
And eies he hadn't seen himself
He snatched from people who had seen 'em.
He gives a glimpse of Sir Walter Raleigh
Not to be found in Lord Macauley;
'Long-faced and sour eie-lidded, a
Kind of pig-eie.'

The strictest pedant can but praise
His brisk and lively observation,
And yet it tempted him at times
To publish idle speculation.
How will the schoolgirl in Wisconsin
Shudder to learn that rare Ben Jonson
'Had one eie lower than t'other, and bigger,
Like Clun the Player; perhaps he begot Clun.'

I heard one tell who heard one tell
Who heard one tell of old John Aubrey
That when he emerged from the Blackmores Head
His eie was rather like a strawberry.

Ogden Nash

The Bright Field

I have seen the sun break through
to illuminate a small field
for a while, and gone my way
and forgotten it. But that was the pearl
of great price, the one field that had
the treasure in it. I realize now
that I must give all that I have
to possess it. Life is not hurrying

on to a receding future, nor hankering after
an imagined past. It is the turning
aside like Moses to the miracle
of the lit bush, to a brightness
that seemed as transitory as your youth
once, but is the eternity that awaits you.

R. S. Thomas

The Little Mute Boy

The little boy was looking for his voice.
(The king of the crickets had it.)
In a drop of water
the little boy was looking for his voice.

I do not want it for speaking with;
I will make a ring of it
that my silence may wear
on its little finger.

In a drop of water
the little boy was looking for his voice.

(The captive voice, far away,
put on a cricket's clothes.)

> Federico García Lorca, translated from
> the Spanish by W. S. Merwin

Fairy Tale

He built himself a house,
    his foundations,
    his stones,
    his walls,
    his roof overhead,
    his chimney and smoke,
    his view from the window.

He made himself a garden,
    his fence,
    his thyme,
    his earthworm,
    his evening dew.

He cut out his bit of sky above.
And he wrapped the garden in the sky
and the house in the garden
and packed the lot in a handkerchief
    and went off
    lone as an arctic fox
    through the cold
    unending
    rain
    into the world.

Miroslav Holub, translated from
the Czech by George Theiner

Sometime we see a cloud that's dragonish;
A vapour sometime like a bear or lion,
A tower'd citadel, a pendant rock,
A forked mountain, or blue promontory
With trees upon't, that nod unto the world
And mock our eyes with air; thou hast seen these signs;
They are black vesper's pageants.'

William Shakespeare, *Antony and Cleopatra*

✴

For me the most terrifying line in Shakespeare comes at the end of this short speech in The Winter's Tale *and is spoken by Leontes, who is wracked with jealousy.*

'How blest am I
In my just censure, in my true opinion!
Alack, for lesser knowledge! How accurs'd
In being so blest! There may be in the cup
A spider steep'd, and one may drink, depart,
And yet partake no venom, for his knowledge
Is not infected; but if one present
The aborr'd ingredient to his eye, make known
How he hath drunk, he cracks his gorge, his sides,
With violent hefts. I have drunk, and seen the spider.'

An oddity: a prophecy, from the Book of Revelation,
chapter 8, verses 10 and 11. Could this refer to 26 April 1986,
or does it lie in the future?

'And the third angel sounded, and there fell a great star
from heaven, burning as it were a lamp, and it fell upon
the third part of the rivers, and upon the fountains of
waters;

'And the name of the star is called Wormwood; and the
third part of the waters became wormwood; and many
men died of the waters, because they were made bitter.'

In Russo/Ukrainian the word for wormwood is: Chernobyl.

The Prophet

With fainting soul athirst for Grace,
I wandered in a desert place,
And at the crossing of the ways
I saw the sixfold seraph blaze;
He touched mine eyes with fingers light
As sleep that cometh in the night:
And like a frighted eagle's eyes,
They opened wide with prophecies.
He touched mine ears, and they were drowned
With tumult and a roaring sound:
I heard convulsion in the sky,
And flights of angel hosts on high,
And beasts that move beneath the sea,
And the sap creeping in the tree.
And bending to my mouth he wrung
From out of it my sinful tongue,
And all its lies and idle rust,
And 'twixt my lips a-perishing
A subtle serpent's forkèd sting
With right hand wet with blood he thrust.
And with his sword my breast he cleft,
My quaking heart thereout he reft,
And in the yawning of my breast
A coal of living fire he pressed.
Then in the desert I lay dead,
And God called unto me and said:
'Arise, and let My voice be heard,
Charged with My Will go forth and span

The land and sea, and let My Word
Lay waste with fire the heart of man.'

Pushkin, translated from the Russian by Maurice Bering

✳

'We are in a world in which "elite" has become an insult,
"discrimination" a swear word, "quality" a joke and
"excellence" an incomprehensible concept. In music it ele-
vates rhythm over melody and mood over feeling, in
literature it encourages lust at the expense of spirit, in
painting it puts colour before expression.'

Bernard Levin

✳

'Almost all absurdity of conduct arises from the imitation
of those we cannot resemble.'

Dr Johnson

✳

'One moon and one only
Is reflected in all waters,
All moons in the water
Are one with the one moon.'

A Zen Buddhist saying

'He who would do good to another must do it in minute particulars. General Good is the plea of the scoundrel, hypocrite and flatterer.'

William Blake

❉

Of the Duke of Wellington, by one of his officers:
'He has nothing of the truncheon about him; nothing foul-mouthed, important, or fussy; his orders on the field are all short, quick, clear, and to the purpose.'

Someone asked Wellington, at a dinner party, what was the most inane remark he had ever heard. His reply – possibly not politically correct – was that before a battle in the Peninsular War he had heard a Portuguese General address his troops saying, 'Remember, men, you are Portuguese.'

❉

'Thence home; and there find one laying of my napkins against tomorrow in figures of all sorts, which is mighty pretty; and it seems it is his trade and he gets much money by it, and doth now and then furnish tables with plate and linen for a feast at so much – which is mighty pretty – and a trade I could not have thought of.'

Samuel Pepys, *Diary*, 13 March 1668

Could this man have been the first caterer brought in to arrange a party?

'On most of her trips Beryl took a pal with her for company, little Gwen Longmire. Little Gwennie's husband, Jack, went to his Reward about two years ago now. Yes, it would be two years since Jack went to his Reward.

'Beryl and Gwen went to New Zealand to boil an egg in a volcano. A Dickens of a long way to go to do a stupid thing like that. Then they went to England for the Changing of the Colour and Buckminster Castle, Anne Hatherley, all that pomp and pageantry. They bought a Polaroid in Singapore for only a fraction more than they would have paid in Melbourne, and there was a bit of my life insurance money left, so they did the Pacific Islands, Manila, Suva, Singapore, Bali; they bought every raffia basket in sight. The Abbos couldn't weave them fast enough.

'But I'm glad I had my Big Trip in my sleep. You see, I wouldn't want to end up in an Eventide Home or a hospital or a Retirement Village or a Twilight Home, smelling of chloroform and Brussels sprouts. That's what they smell like to me. Death and roast dinner. Gravy and the grave. You go into one of these hospitals to see your loved ones. You know they are not coming home. The sisters tip you the wink. You're sitting on the edge of their bed, trying not to look in their locker, and you're saying, "No, no, those grapes are for *you*. All right, just one." You leave them with a few twigs. And you say to them, "We've kept your lovely room just as you left it." You've let it to an Asian student but you don't tell them that. And he's bringing his family out next week. And you're looking at them, wondering if they know you.

And they're looking up at you, wondering if you know they know you know. They know, you know.'

Barry Humphries, *Shades of Sandy Stone*

✳

The last words of the novelist Henry James are reported to have been: 'Ah, here it comes, the Distinguished Thing.'

✳

The great theatre director, and my very good friend, Tyrone Guthrie, on returning from a visit to Los Angeles, gave me a description of the office building of the Music Corporation of America — the giant theatrical agency of the Forties and Fifties.

'I want you to imagine', he said, 'a long, whitewashed, two-storeyed cottage. Got that?'

'Yes,' I replied.

'Now put lovely dark green shutters on either side of every window.'

'Done,' I said.

'Put on a Spanish tiled roof; and now cover the whole thing with pink rambler roses. Have you done that?'

'Yes, fairly well,' I said.

'Now' — and he drew a big breath — 'enlarge the whole thing to ten times the size of St Pancras Station.'

'In this time Our Lord showed a little thing, the quantity of an hazelnut, in the palm of my hand; and it was as round as a ball. I looked there upon with eye of my understanding, and thought: "What may this be?" And it was generally answered thus: "It is all that is made." I marvelled how it might last, for methought it might suddenly have fallen to nought for littleness. And I was answered in my understanding: "It lasteth, and ever shall last for that God loveth it." And so all thing hath the Being by the love of God.

'In this little thing I saw three properties. The first is that God made it; the second is that God loveth it; the third that God keepeth it. But what is to me soothly the Maker, the Keeper, the Lover, – I cannot tell.'

Julian of Norwich, *Revelations of Divine Love*, 8 May 1373

❋

'O mighty Nothing! unto thee,
Nothing, we owe all things that be:
God spake once when he all things made,
He saved all when he *Nothing* said.
The world was made of *Nothing* then;
'Tis made by *Nothing* now again.'

Richard Crashaw, 'And he answered them nothing',
Steps to the Temple

A letter giving a lower-deck view of the Battle of Trafalgar from the Royal Sovereign.

Honoured Father,

This comes to tell you I am alive and hearty except three fingers; but that's not much, it might have been my head. I told brother Tom I should like to see a greadly battle, and I have seen one, and we have peppered the Combined rarely; and for the matter of that, they fought us pretty tightish for French and Spanish. Three of our mess are killed, and four more of us winged. But to tell you the truth of it, when the game began, I wished myself at Warnborough with my plough again; but when they had given us one duster, and I found myself snug and tight, I set to in good earnest, and thought no more about being killed than if I were at Murrell Green Fair, and I was presently as busy and as black as a collier. How my fingers got knocked overboard I don't know, but off they are, and I never missed them till I wanted them. You see, by my writing, it was my left hand, so I can write to you and fight for my King yet. We have taken a rare parcel of ships, but the wind is so rough we cannot bring them home, else I should roll in money, so we are busy smashing 'em, and blowing 'em up wholesale.

Our dear Admiral Nelson is killed! So we have paid pretty sharply for licking 'em. I never set eyes on him, for which I am both sorry and glad, for, to be sure, I should like to have seen him – but then, all the men in our ship who have seen him are such soft toads, they have done nothing but blast their eyes, and cry, ever since he was killed. God bless you! Chaps that fought like the devil sit down and cry like a wench. I am still in the *Royal Sovereign*, but the Admiral [Collingwood] has left her, for she is like a horse without a bridle, so he is in a frigate that he may be here and there and everywhere, for he's as *cute* as here and there one, and as bold as a lion, for all he can cry! – I saw his tears with my own eyes, when the boat hailed and said my lord was dead. So no more at present from your dutiful son,

Sam

E. Hallam Moorhouse (ed.), *Letters of the English Seamen*

✷

At the age of fourteen, the future Captain Marryat was taken to see Nelson's funeral in January 1806. He wrote of it:

'As the triumphal car disappeared from my aching eye, I felt that death could have no terrors if followed by such a funeral; and I determined that I would be buried in the same manner.'

From Peter Simple *by Captain Marryat, which recounts a ball given in Barbados, circa 1814:*

'It was my fate to sit opposite a fine turkey, and I asked my partner if I should have the pleasure of helping her to a piece of the breast. She looked at me very indignantly, and said, "Curse your impudence, Sar, I wonder where you learn manners. Sar, I take a lilly turkey *bosom*, if you please. Talk of *breast* to a lady, Sar – really quite horrid." '

Another Dog's Death

For days the good old bitch had been dying, her back
pinched down to the spine and arched to ease the pain,
   her kidneys dry, her muzzle white. At last
I took a shovel into the woods and dug her grave

in preparation for the certain. She came along,
which I had not expected. Still, the children gone,
   such expeditions were rare, and the dog,
spayed early, knew no nonhuman word for love.

She made her stiff legs trot and let her bent tail wag.
We found a spot we liked, where the pines met the field.
   The sun warmed her fur as she dozed and I dug;
I carved her a safe place while she protected me.

I measured her length with the shovel's long handle;
she perked in amusement, and sniffed the heaped-up earth.
   Back down at the house, she seemed friskier, but
gagged, eating. We called the vet a few days later.

They were old friends. She held up a paw, and he
injected a violet fluid. She swooned on the lawn;
   we watched her breathing quickly slow and cease.
In the wheelbarrow up to the hole, her fur took the sun.

   John Updike

Walking Away

It is eighteen years, almost to the day —
A sunny day with the leaves just turning,
The touch-lines new-ruled — since I watched you play
Your first game of football, then, like a satellite
Wrenched from its orbit, go drifting away

Behind a scatter of boys. I can see
You walking away from me towards the school
With the pathos of a half-fledged thing set free
Into the wilderness, the gait of one
Who finds no path where the path should be.

That hesitant figure, eddying away
Like a winged seed loosened from its parent stem,
Has something I never quite grasp to convey
About nature's give-and-take — the small, the scorching
Ordeals which fire one's irresolute clay.

I have had worse partings, but none that so
Gnaws at my mind still. Perhaps it is roughly
Saying what God alone could perfectly show —
How selfhood begins with a walking away,
And love is proved in the letting go.

  C. Day Lewis

The old elevated railway in New York, known familiarly as
the 'El', stood almost thirty feet above street level, and was a
joy to ride, because you could peer into people's bedrooms,
and so on. When it was demolished much of the ironwork was
sold, I understand, to the Japanese.

plato told

him:he couldn't
believe it(jesus

told him;he
wouldn't believe
it)lao

tsze
certainly told
him,and general
(yes

mam)
sherman;
and even
(believe it
or

not)you
told him:i told
him;we told him
(he didn't believe it,no

sir)it took
a nipponized bit of
the old sixth

avenue
el;in the top of his head:to tell

him

E. E. Cummings

The Roman Centurion's Song

Legate, I had the news last night – my cohort ordered home
By ship to Portus Itius and thence by road to Rome.
I've marched the companies aboard, the arms are stowed
    below:
Now let another take my sword. Command me not to go!

I've served in Britain forty years, from Vectis to the Wall.
I have none other home than this, nor any life at all.
Last night I did not understand, but, now the hour draws
    near
That calls me to my native land, I feel that land is here.

Here where men say my name was made, here where my
    work was done;
Here where my dearest dead are laid – my wife – my wife
    and son;
Here, where time, custom, grief and toil, age, memory,
    service, love,
Have rooted me in British soil. Ah, how can I remove?

For me this land, that sea, these airs, those folk and fields
    suffice.
What purple Southern pomp can match our changeful
    Northern skies,
Black with December snows unshed or pearled with
    Autumn haze –
The changing arch of steel-grey March, or June's
    long-lighted days?

You'll follow widening Rhodanus till vine and olive
    lean
Aslant before the sunny breeze that sweeps Nemausus
    clean
To Arelate's triple gate; but let me linger on,
Here where our stiff-necked British oaks confront
    Euroclydon!

You'll take the old Aurelian Road through
    shore-descending pines
Where, blue as any peacock's neck, the Tyrrhene Ocean
    shines.
You'll go where laurel crowns are worn, but — will you
    e'er forget
The scent of hawthorn in the sun, or bracken in the
    wet?

Let me work here for Britain's sake — at any task you
    will —
A marsh to drain, a road to make or native troops to
    drill.
Some Western camp (I know the Pict) or granite Border
    keep,
Mid seas of heather derelict, where our old messmates
    sleep.

Legate, I come to you in tears — My cohort ordered
    home!
I've served in Britain forty years. What should I do in
    Rome?

Here is my heart, my soul, my mind – the only life I
   know.
I cannot leave it all behind. Command me not to go!

   Rudyard Kipling

Titles for two books – or for two halves of one book?
Hawthorn in the Sun/Bracken in the Wet

❈

Two exit lines from Act V of Love's Labours Lost:

'Keep some state in thy exit, and vanish.'

'The words of Mercury are harsh after the songs of
Apollo. You that way, we this way.'

❈

*A Catholic Bishop (Western Isles? Argyllshire?) – recounted
to me by Fr Nugent S.J. – said, 'We once had a Conservative
candidate for the Isle of Burra. He told the islanders that if
returned he would bring work to the islands. Naturally he lost
his deposit.'*

❈

Little Dorrit *party at Rotherhithe. Tall elderly man placed
his shrimp heads and tails on my cardboard plate of chicken
and veg, and then asked me, 'What's this party all about?'*

New enthusiasms in old age:
> *Lady Herbert taking up chess and off to the tournament*
> *in Eastbourne.*
> *Dorothy Samuels discovering Chaucer and becoming*
> *something of an expert.*
> *Grandma Moses.*
> *Old people taking university degrees.*

✴

Peter's Pence, Peter's Pounds. Started late eighth century.
Abolished by Henry VIII — Defender of the Faith.

✴

'. . . and love to Richard
Is a strange brooch in this all-hating world.'
> William Shakespeare, *Richard II*

✴

Pornographic literature vividly colours the mind and clouds
the spirit.

✴

'You ha' freshed my rememory.'
> Ben Jonson, *A Tale of a Tub*

✴

'By conscious art practised with natural ease.'
> T. S. Eliot, 'To Walter de la Mare'

'. . . mock me all over,
From my flat cap, unto my shining shoes.'

Ben Jonson, *Every Man in His Humour*

❋

HELENA: 'Fie, fie! You counterfeit! You puppet, you!'
HERMIA: 'Puppet! Why so? Ay, that way goes the game!
Now I perceive that she hath made compare
Between our statures; she hath urg'd her height;
And with her personage, her tall personage,
Her height, forsooth, she hath prevail'd with him.
And are you grown so high in his esteem
Because I am so dwarfish and so low?
How low am I, thou painted maypole? Speak:
How low am I?'

William Shakespeare, *A Midsummer Night's Dream*

❋

*A hot summer evening, drinks time. I put on a compact disc
of Brendel playing Haydn sonatas. Lady guest: 'Oh, how
lovely! Just the time to listen to music!' Picking up a copy of
the* Spectator, *'Now, what do you think is going to happen in
China?'*

❋

*At the National Theatre, July 1989
I was accosted when going into the auditorium by a gross, glittering, squat American woman, who shrieked, 'Oh, my
Guard! My Guard! Fancy seeing you here! And in your very
own theatre, Mr Olivier!'*

45

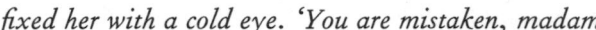

my guard!

*I fixed her with a cold eye. 'You are mistaken, madam.
Mr Olivier died last week.'*

She pealed with laughter and continued, 'But I know *you!
I* know *I* know *you! Who are you?'*

I made my way to my seat sedately.

＊

Half-waking thoughts on Hamlet; *troubled sleep because of
violently noisy barbecue party a mile or more away; the
windows wide open because of stifling heat.*
'What does this mean, my lord?'
*'The King doth wake tonight and takes his rouse,
Keeps wassail and the swaggering up-spring reels,
And as he drains his draughts of Rhenish down
The kettle-drum and trumpet thus bray out
The triumph of his pledge.'*

46

During 'My tables — meet it is I set it down', etc., presumably Hamlet writes: '"Adieu, adieu! Remember me."' When in Act II Scene 2, he enters reading, and encounters Polonius, should he be reading from his 'tables'? Perhaps again — but very doubtfully — when he enters for 'To be, or not to be'?

In taking, or looking at, Ophelia's prayer book, would it be good to indicate she has had the book upside down? And at the end of Act II Scene 2 — 'You could, for a need, study a speech of some dozen or sixteen lines which I would set down and insert in't, could you not?' — perhaps he could start to write in the 'tables' again, even before 'O what a rogue', etc. and after 'Now I am alone.' Don't know.

Richard Eyre's production at the National divided the play into two, the first part running two and a half hours up until Hamlet's departure for England, at the end of his final soliloquy. The second part ran one and a half hours. The play is not too long, uncut, but that division puts a strain on audience and actors.

I now think that it needs presenting in five acts, as printed and, probably, as written. After all, in a symphony you expect a short breather between movements, to shift your behind and legs, clear your throat, etc. This endless running of one scene into another, non-stop, derives I think from the cinema. It creates a fake sense of pace.

My scheme would enable a fifteen-second pause in the playing after 'O cursed spite/That ever I was born to set it right!/Nay, come, let's go together.'

A short interval after 'The play's the thing?/Wherein I'll
catch the conscience of the king.'
　　Another fifteen seconds after 'Good night, mother'.
　　An interval after the King's 'Let's follow, Gertrude . . .
Therefore let's follow.'
　　These are all minor finales. And Hamlet himself would be
given a long rest before the grave scene and the fight.

✳

Middle-aged manicurist at Trumpers; red-golden hair, black
at the roots; had a sort of nervous charm. Shook her head viol-
ently from side to side in time with filing my nails. She'll end
up with severe neck trouble.

✳

Streaks of sunlight, at regular intervals, slanting through a
leafless hedge, striking the trunks of plane trees, making
them look a vivid green; and where they landed on lime trees
a glowing black.

✳

I neither suffer myself, nor other fools, gladly.

✳

'The good not done, the love not given, time
Torn off unused.'
　　Philip Larkin, 'Aubade'

Leaving the Wellington Hospital, Saturday evening, 19 September 1993, after visiting Merula, I was approached by two Canadian girls. They were quite jolly and sweet, aged twenty-three and twenty-nine, and they asked me the way 'down town'. They wanted to visit a pub and have a meal. I said I would give them a lift in a taxi if we found one. We had to walk to Baker Street before we were successful. As we passed the mosque I said, 'That's the new mosque.' 'What's a mosque?' they asked. I explained; they looked dumb. One worked in computers, the other in advertising films. They came from Toronto. Had I ever been to Canada? Yes, to Toronto, Quebec and Stratford, Ontario. They had never heard of the theatre there; but they were abysmally ignorant of everything. They told me that they were at the start of a European tour. Where? They weren't sure. Paris, France, might be nice; Italy, Germany, Venice, Rome — they could do it in a week. I dropped them at Covent Garden. They sweetly offered — but I declined — their share of the fare. I returned to the Connaught slightly amused and yet rather sad.

✳

*Coleridge's 'To see him [Kean] act is like reading Shakespeare by flashes of lightning' (*Table Talk*). I prefer a steady light. In Kean's case was it Dickens's 'bottled lightning'?*

An excellent and amusing article in the Evening Standard
*on musical conductors who talk too much, and pretentiously,
at their orchestras. One musician says, 'All we need to be told
is fast, slow, loud or quiet.'*

⁂

Quote from a Sunday Telegraph *interview with Nicholas
Craig:*

'When he plays Wilde, his demands are no less stringent.
He cites the following example from *The Importance*:
" 'My dear Algy, I thought you were down in Shropshire.
How ripping to find that you are up instead.' What is it
like to have a friend called Algy? Ask around. Better still,

look through the phone book and find someone called
Algy. Get to know him. *Befriend* him. *Go* to Shropshire.
Find out why it is so ripping not to be there. *Live the line.*
The audience haven't paid to see people walking about in
nice costumes saying amusing things, they want 'other
being', they want *rawness*, they want 'the truth'."'

*What balls-aching balderdash! Enough to bring on a heart
attack. I wonder how much Wilde would have appreciated
rawness. George Alexander would have been spared, at least,
'the phone book'.*

✳

*I have a friend (female, a few months younger than me) who
thinks it vulgar to mention age. But we start doing so very
early on. 'I am six and three quarters,' we say, when we have
barely reached six and a half. And then, when the years have
lengthened, we proudly announce we are seventy-five. Who
the hell is going to say, 'You don't look a day over fifty'? No
one I know. Eighty is the tricky time, I imagine; old actors
start saying they are nearly ninety, hoping for sympathy,
admiration and astonishment that they can still put one foot
in front of another or remember a line. Ernest Thesiger, the
eccentric, high-camp English actor, claimed that another old
actor, A. E. Matthews, was the same age as himself but had
added a decade to his years to appear more important.*

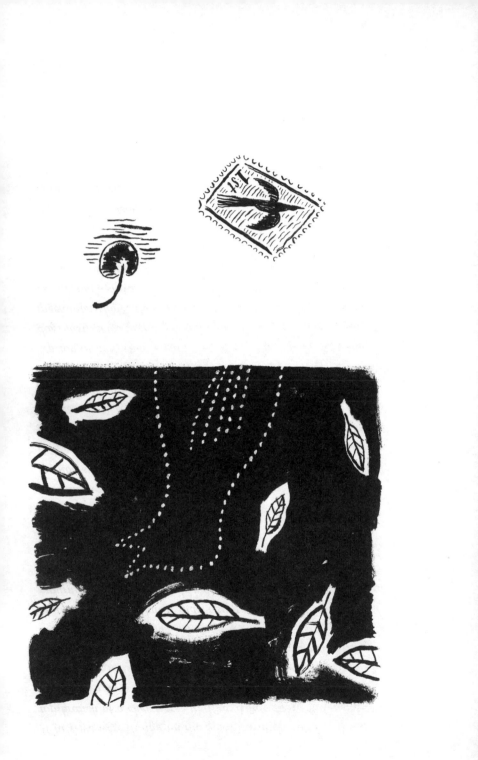

While we were dining on the patio a small warbler sat on the top branch of a cherry tree and gave delightful and insistent voice. Two days later I found a dead warbler on the balcony; presumably it had dashed itself against a window. When I picked it up its flattened little corpse seemed to weigh no more than a postage stamp. Last night there was a warbler again on the cherry tree, but it didn't sing. A husband? Wife? A mourning friend? Do birds have friends? I think I have heard of deep friendship between a duck and a goose.

✷

When I was a young, enthusiastic theatre-goer, but before becoming a professional actor, I often heard people — members of audiences or people who pretended to theatrical judgement or sophistication — say of some actress or other, 'I so admire her technique.*' I never knew what they were talking about, which shamed me.*

I still don't know. When I watch, say, Maggie Smith, I have no awareness of any 'technical' accomplishment, no perception of any wheels which may be going round; what she does just seems to me mesmeric and true. If the 'technique' or mechanics show, then there must be something wrong. In any case I don't want *to know; I just want to believe, enjoy and be taken into another world.*

✷

Ralph Richardson, with me on his arm, entering a grand hotel in Zurich and saying to the maître d', 'Two tables, please'.

St Mary's Church, Cadogan Street. Upright, splendid-looking old man, probably in his mid eighties, sitting in a pew waiting to go to confession. Marvellous expression of dignity and kindliness written on his face. When he stood and picked up his cap I realized he was a Chelsea Pensioner.

✳

Two nuns got on the cog-wheel railway at Vitznau to go up Mt Rigi. Only one came down. Can we take it that the other was assumed?

✳

A mad semi-waking dream from a nap: a production of Lear *in which the storm scenes were played by marionettes manipulated by the actors. Something to do with the gods playing with tiny men.*

It is strange how often I have dreamed – and subsequently thought – about bizarre productions of Lear*. A few years ago I was obsessed with the idea of presenting* Lear *as Tolstoy – the mad scenes set on a deserted railway station, the storm the sound of great steam engines thundering through. Then there was my original* Lear *dream when Larry asked me to play the Fool, and I saw the Fool, white faced, with only one eyebrow, standing at the end of the bed. I said to Larry I would play it if I could carry out my dream. Which I did. Larry didn't like the idea but kept his promise. As the storm went on I streaked off most of my make-up, and finally all. Perhaps it was a wrong conception and too elaborate, but I feel that when dreams present themselves vigorously they*

*have to be fulfilled. The Fool was my first real success in the
theatre.*

✻

*Tourist guides – mostly women – in The Mall, holding up
dumpy furled umbrellas like torches, leading groups of twenty
or so people. Sometimes the groups criss-crossing each other or
intermingling. An idea for the opening of a comedy film –
following the wrong umbrellas.
   Tourist buses, painted with grizzly, facetious horror scenes
and blaring misinformation. London is being turned into a
horrendous 'theme park'.*

✻

*Are halcyon days only in winter?
I think so.*

✻

*Last Friday, 5 May, private lunch party at Sotheby's. Sat
between Lady Charteris (wife of the Provost of Eton) and my
hostess, Miss Pullers. Liked them both. Talked mostly with
Lady C and found her amusing. She glanced at my place
card and said, 'Theatre! I hope you didn't like that boring
and disgusting play,* Waiting for Godot. *I so disliked it I
haven't been to the theatre since – about twenty-five years.
And I don't like T. S. Eliot's plays either.' And then I think
she said 'Crap!' but as she was looking at her plate at that
moment the word may have been 'crub'. I decided she was the
Queen of the Philistines, but bright, good-natured and
charming.*

The pale weak wrists of most priests; the strong left legs of all genuflecting Catholics.

✳

A nightmare, half-awake, of trudging through a deep tunnel from Sam Wanamaker's Globe Theatre (yet to be constructed) to the site of the Rose Theatre. Sprinklers to keep the ground foul and muddy, but Government over-shoes supplied free. Piped Elizabethan music interspersed with one-liners from Shakespeare. The scent of Shakespeare's flowers wafted, hotly, out of black and corroded tubes. At the half-way point an inserted window showing scenes from The Jew of Malta *(twice defaced, once by Israelis and once by Palestinians) and a scene from* Tamburlaine *covered with 'No Popery' graffiti. A poster of* Hero and Leander, *showing*

Neptune making lascivious advances to Leander swimming
across the Hellespont, carried a government AIDS warning.
Arriving at the entrance to the Rose saw a public-relations
scheme to raise money: 'Record for posterity a Mighty
Line from Marlowe. £1000 must be won. Recording fee
£1.99. Judges will be Mr Edward Heath and Dame Vera
Lynn.'

❋

On Corpus Christi, just as I was about to leave St Mary's,
Cadogan St, after 8 a.m. Mass, a thin woman in an Irish-
green dress handed me a 'missalette' to autograph. 'I've got
Kenneth Williams and John Cleese,' she said. 'I won't sign
autographs in church,' I replied, 'and anyway not on a mis-
sal.' She followed me into the porch, rummaged in a bag,
and produced a doctor's bill. 'This'll do,' she said. 'He won't
mind.'

❋

In Simpson's, Piccadilly, men's suits department. Overheard
an elderly foreign salesman on the telephone: 'Patricia, can
you give me the words for "Auld Lang Syne"? I know the
tune.' (He hummed it unrecognizably.) 'You can't? Oh dear!
What am I to do?' I said, over my shoulder, 'We'll take a
cup of kindness yet, etc.' Another salesman, whom I
hadn't noticed, said, 'I beg your pardon, sir?' No use
explaining.

A late middle-aged workman, sipping beer outside a pub in Elizabeth Street. I didn't catch what he said to his mate except, pointing indignantly with a little finger at a white van, 'That's the bugger. You can smell him a mile off.'

✳

The popping cracking noise of a cube of ice falling into water.

✳

The strength *of dry Martinis in NY – anyway in the Forties and Fifties. Made without ice, the jug of gin and wisp of vermouth was placed in the freezer a few hours before one drank. Lethal.*

✳

I like the sound of many things, but not the barking of dogs, the road drill or the hovering, inquisitive helicopter.

*'I hope I have a sense of humour,' she said. A disastrous
admission of having none.*

✳

*A confessional at St Richard's Church, Chichester. A small
room with a prie-dieu against a screen; couldn't see the priest
except from his knees down; his ankles crossed, thick grey
socks and sandals. A very relaxed position, too casual for
administering the sacrament of penance. But it was a very hot
day. No word of greeting or encouragement. A long silence
after my confession. Was he asleep? No, a cold voice finally
came out with a platitude or two and poor, brief advice. Still,
greatly preferable to confession in a Franciscan church in New
York where I could clearly see, through the grille, that the
young priest was masturbating. Not stimulated by anything I
had said, I am sure.*

✳

'Here we sung several good things, but I am more and
more confirmed that singing with many voices is not singing, but a sort of Instrumental music, the sense of the
words being lost by not being heard, and especially as
they set them with Fuges of words, one after another;
whereas singing properly, I think, should be but with one
or two voices at most, and that counterpoint.'
Samuel Pepys, *Diary*, 15 September 1667

59

'I'll deliver all;
And promise you calm seas, auspicious gales . . .'
   William Shakespeare, *The Tempest*

⁂

*The heavy, springless tread across the floor, with the tiny
stagger, when you get up in the dark of night.*

⁂

*Lapsang souchong: I like it a
lot (anyway with a pinch of
Darjeeling) but it does smell
like kipper skins or bloater
paste — with a touch of
creosote.*

*A man knocked over by a van in Oxford Street — just a few
yards behind me, as I was turning towards Soho Square. I
didn't see the impact but the scrunch of breaks brought my
head round and I saw his head hit the curb of the pavement.*

A sickening crack. He was probably killed. Oxford Street was crowded, as usual, and what surprised me was the curious sound people made: not shrieks, shouts or cries but a sort of twittering like a flock of frightened small birds. Very eerie. We were all thinking, I suppose, of sudden accidental death. Thoughts of death lingered in my mind for days.

✷

From the Berry Bros & Rudd wine list:
'This superb Brunello shows classic breeding with a touch of austerity.'

✷

Strange semi-waking dreams about Twelfth Night. *There is something to be worked out, particularly in the early scenes, between Viola and Sebastian, as to which actor plays which. On the assumption that both actor and actress – or both actors – can look* very *alike (it would be wonderful if they were twins, of course) and are dressed identically, possibly in black with a little relief, and Sebastian's jacket perhaps a bit sea-worn, then I would like to see the following experiment:*

 Act I Sc 2: Viola played by Viola – in women's clothes.
 Act I Sc 4: Cesario (Viola) – played by Sebastian –
  but not *in worn jacket.*
 Act I Sc 5: Viola played by Sebastian as in Act I Sc 4.
 Act II Sc I: Sebastian – played by Sebastian (in worn coat).
 Act II Sc 2: Viola – played by Viola.
 Act II Sc 4: Viola – played by Viola.

Act III Sc 1: Viola – played by Sebastian
Act III Sc 3: Sebastian – played by Sebastian
From then on as in the text – I think. I believe that the
early acceptance *(by the other characters) of either Viola or*
Sebastian being whom it is assumed they are will pay strong
dividends at the end of the play. And if *there is one obvious*
discrepancy in face or figure between the two of them then
audiences and cast can together sing, 'Well, we were deceived
throughout.' It all seemed rather exhilarating and almost
important in the darkness of night; now it looks pretty feeble
and finicky.

*

Polonius – spying:

'If it be so, as so 'tis put on me
And that in way of caution . . .'

'You shall do marvellous wisely, good Reynaldo,
Before you visit him, to make inquire
Of his behaviour.'

  'I will find
Where truth is hid, though it were hid indeed
Within the centre.'

'Be you and I behind an arras then.
Mark the encounter.'

'My lord, he's going to his mother's closet.
Behind the arras I'll convey myself
To hear the process.'

'I'll silence me e'en here.'

William Shakespeare, *Hamlet*

✻

'Like many men who always see two sides to a question,
he loved to discharge his conscience by leaning on the
counsel of those who saw only one.'

Ronald Knox, *Barchester Pilgrimage*

✻

'I wonder what day I shall die on –
One passes year by year over one's death day,
As one might pass over one's grave.'

Cardinal Newman

✻

'And duller shouldst thou be than the fat weed
That roots itself in ease on Lethe wharf,
Wouldst thou not stir in this.'

William Shakespeare, *Hamlet*

'I rather would entreat thy company
To see the wonders of the world abroad,
Than, living dully sluggardis'd at home,
Wear out thy youth with shapeless idleness.'

    William Shakespeare, *The Two Gentlemen of Verona*

✳

'The child's ball was beautiful. Near one hundred of
them, neither crowd nor heat. The King was engrossed
with the Bedford children. He saw one of her boys looking at his order of the Golden Fleece, and asked him what
he thought that order was. "Chinese I suppose." We did
not look quite pleased.'

    Harriet Grenville, *A Second Self* (letters), 3 January 1824

✳

*Yesterday a beautiful, black, young woman taxi-driver drove
me, swiftly and admirably, from Fulham Road to the Connaught. She had a Rastafarian hairdo.*

✳

'"Ha!" I said. And I meant it to sting.'

    P. G. Wodehouse, *Very Good, Jeeves*

✳

*Awake in the night, I had an image of the Porter in Mac-
beth. The knocking at the 'south entry' was rapid and far
from thunderous. Then the voice of the Porter was sort of
muffled. He made his entrance putting on a shirt so that his
head was still inside it and the sleeves dangling up in the air*

– a struggling sort of ghost. Could be both funny and frighten-
ing. When we next see Macbeth he is in his nightshirt –
having struggled quickly into it.

Later, perhaps his movements across the stage might fol-
low the same pattern as Macbeth's following the dagger, etc.

✻

'"Do you remember what I said to you long ago . . . ?"
'The smile with which he met this appeal was not, it
was to be feared, robust. "What haven't you, love, said in
your time?"'

Henry James, *The Golden Bowl*

✻

A dark, large, wasp-like creature climbing round my study
window; suggested an articulated lorry.

✻

Strange half-waking dream last night – well, speculation
really – about the hidden years of Christ from, say, fourteen
to thirty. Robert Graves suggested they were spent in Rome.
Someone else that he went to Persia and India (more likely).
I don't find much to interest me in the accepted carpenter-shop
life in Nazareth. Why no tale or memory of such a vivid per-
sonality among a tale-bearing people? My dream concerned
the parable of the Prodigal Son. Apart from the unacceptable
– presumably – life spent with harlots, etc., was it a fictional
work-up of his own story? And, if it possibly could be, would
the return coincide with Joseph's death, for instance, leaving
Mary a widow? Joseph is clearly out the picture, probably

ad, by the time Christ starts his mission — which seems psychologically right.

※

New words or meanings, done to death in the past few weeks: 'squeaky clean' and 'forecourt' (for petrol station).

※

Her telephone-answering machine went on giving her number, in her bright encouraging voice, and saying she would call back as soon as possible, for days after she was dead.

※

Camera operator Kafka *very pleasant and waggish. 'Yeah! It's Welwyn Garden City' for something being well in shot. And of the young focus-puller, draped in a piece of black material, 'You look like a* Homo sapiens*' — for 'queer', presumably.*

※

Walked in grounds in afternoon. A cold wind, bright sun. A lot of fallen leaves. Smells of sea on the wind and mushrooms underfoot. Rather heady.

※

Somewhere in the middle of Rabbit at Rest *a character says, in effect, that we live in a thin skin of light wrapped around a ball of darkness. Something like that. How to answer it, if an answer is necessary? All that comes to mind is Vaughan's*

'There is in God – some say –
A deep, but dazzling darkness; as men here
Say it is late and dusky, because they
   See not all clear.'

✳

*A fleshy old man, moving from room to room, apparently
pausing to admire pictures and objects, but in fact quietly eas-
ing out a little gas at each stop so as not to startle the hushed
tapestried world around him with a resounding fart.*

✳

'To believe in God is not a decision that we can make. All
we can do is decide not to give our love to false gods.'
   Simone Weil

✳

*I detect in myself a regular, daily, increased appreciation of
trees, the look of things, even the weather (whatever it is). Is
this a premonition of mortality?*

✳

'He that is himself weary will soon weary the public. Let him
therefore lay down his employment whatever it may be, who
can no longer assert his former activity or attention; let him
not endeavour to struggle with censure, or deliberately infest
the stage until a general hiss commands him to depart.'
   Dr Johnson

Press photograph of swimmers in rubber caps, their mouths wide open, crawling through the water of public baths; you can smell the chlorine. Press photographs of cricketers' turns as they twist to complete a shot to leg. Press photos of footballers colliding in the air and rugger players on top of each other on the muddy ground. A smell of wet leather and sweet crushed grass.

✳

Longtailed tits, clustered all around a cylinder of nuts, their black tails jutting out, looked like an old-fashioned chimney-sweep's brush.

✳

Merula lay on the sofa in front of the fire, reading in an absorbed way. Outside the sitting-room window fine snow fell slowly and steadily. 'I'm going out,' I said. She didn't look up. 'Just down to the post. I may be gone some time,' I said in a voice of fatality. Still she didn't look up. So I squeaked across the floor in my rubberized boots and slithered down the drive with a few unimportant letters.

✳

'Sloth aspireth to a kind of quietness; yet where is true repose but in our Lord?'
St Augustine, *Confessions*

✳

'And they shall die suddenly and be deprived of all their kindred, and leave their brave attire strewn upon the earth – conducted in this manner, the judgement will be just

'. . . I have made my sons judges . . . And these, when they are dead, shall give judgement in the meadow at the parting of the ways, whence the two roads lead, one to the Islands of the Blessed, and the other to Tartarus.'

Plato, *Gorgias*

✳

'The three most important things a man has are, briefly, his private parts, his money, and his religious opinions.'

Samuel Butler

I am tempted to add: the first two diminish with age and only the last is rigid.

✳

Seen in Bond Street
Eight stalwart workers carrying, with difficulty, a big metal angel with vast wings. They carried it face down towards a waiting lorry, shuffling and stopping every step or two. Suddenly they broke into song – the 'Song of the Volga Boatmen'.

Of Masques and Triumphs:
'The colours that show best by candlelight are white,
carnation, and a kind of sea-water green.'

Francis Bacon, *Essays*

Night Thoughts

*After hearing Keith Waterhouse, on TV, say the moral rot
set in when one ceased to fear chair attendants in the park.*

*(What has happened to all the
little collapsible green chairs in
Hyde Park, which used to stand
around in twos and threes before
deckchairs became the norm?
Perhaps they are still there, but
dispersed. I must go and look.)
And the rowing skiffs and var-
nished rowing boats on the
Serpentine have been (mostly?)*
*replaced by brightly coloured tubby rowboats as if at a seaside
theme park. I think I'd put back our moral decline to the dis-
appearance of horse-drawn traffic on the London roads. There*

was a nobility in the old dray horse, gazing with large moist eyes at pedestrians. And good sense and humility in the sweepers who cleared up the precious manure. Another lapse from moral certitudes probably came with the dial telephone, which has led to hoax alarm calls and indifference to wrong numbers.

Take-away food is another dispiriting sign of moral and family collapse. Now the tired pizza, hard as thick cardboard, instead of the warm, floppy, greasy piece of newspaper in which nestled lovely potato chips soured with vinegar and salt, something you could offer to friends as you walked in the streets. 'Wanna bite of my pizza?' is not the same.

Dipping deep into a well of loneliness and bringing up a dry bucket of sterility. Colonel Barker in the late Twenties marrying a vacuously innocent girl. I always wondered how it worked, or when was the moment of Mrs Barker's awakening. No designer stubble on the Colonel; I see her smooth round face, monocle in eye, warming a large hippy rump in front of a seaside hotel's smoking fire, a jolly good gin-and-it in her hand, and possibly choking on a cigar. Oh, the sadness, almost eclipsing the gaiety of nations.

The signs of the times could be read, decades ago, in the

made-up bow tie. One should have been able to see the Angli-can bishop, rustling in a long magenta frock, flashing an

emerald ring, accompanied by his beautiful curly-haired chap-lain (male, still) and the chap-lain's lifelong companion. A ménage à trois. 'Where shall we three meet again?' At another of Lady Hartwell's election-night parties.

Could the admirable Mr Major be referred to by the media as 'the Prime Minister' and not as 'the Prime Minister, Mr Major', as if we didn't know his name? After all, the previous occupant of No. 10 was usually referred to either as 'Mrs Thatcher' or 'the Prime Minister'; whichever came first, neither her name nor position had to be explained. And in exchange for the media courtesy could Mr Major (while Prime Minister) avoid keeping his hands in his pockets when speaking — it makes him look like the most popular and over-confident prefect in the school. If he can't resist the hands-in-his-pockets pose, Mr Major should sew the pockets up — the mild punishment that used to be meted out to shuffling schoolboys and sloppy actors who didn't know what to do with their hands. The Duke of Edinburgh and the Prince of Wales have compromised on 'what to do with hands' by putting theirs behind their backs. Out of sight, out of mind. The Queen, of course, has a handbag — a useful weapon.

In the night reflected, a little sourly but with some amuse-
ment, on the ghastliness of some fans and the venom of their
revenge when they feel thwarted. Edith Hargreaves (?) was a
large, fleshy-nosed, white-faced fan of Edith Evans and
looked like a surburban caricature of her. A sort of companion
and dresser to Edith, whom she deserted to be Michael Red-
grave's dresser and minder. When she came into money
(twice) she loaded the Redgraves with huge unwanted gifts,
like radiograms. Then, when I first played Hamlet, *at Bux-*
ton, there was a plump young woman who wrote me sonnets
about my performance — 'cool fingers of the rain', etc., etc.
These were more or less ignored by me — cruelly, I suppose.
She had her revenge when, years later, she edited The
Oxford Book of the Theatre, *dismissing my name in a*
couple of lines. Then there was old Alfred Parker, whom, acci-
dentally, I kept waiting too long at my dressing-room door
during The Old Country. *He wrote a vicious letter about my*
conceit and snobbery. I wouldn't have hurt him for the world
and, indeed, had given him the tickets for the show. But burn-
ing underneath the fan-like enthusiasm was camp, sibilant,
would-be ownership and jealousy. I had been remembering all
this when I came across Samuel Butler's sonnet about his
devoted Miss Eliza Savage, who turned on him:

'She was too kind, wooed too persistently,
Wrote moving letters to me day by day;
The more she wrote, the more unmoved was I,
The more she gave, the less could I repay.'

'Here is a play fitted'

'And we may rehearse most obscenely and courageously.
Take pains, be perfect.'

BOTTOM: 'Are we all met?'
QUINCE: 'Pat, pat; and here's a marvellous convenient
place for our rehearsal.'

'You speak all your part at once, cues, and all.'

'And most dear actors, eat no onions nor garlic, for we
are to utter sweet breath.'

'The battle with the Centaurs, to be sung
By an Athenian's eunuch to the harp!
We'll none of that.'

William Shakespeare, *A Midsummer Night's Dream*

'[It] will be quite clear to the reader, who must soon perceive great inexperience, immaturity, and every error denoting a feverish attempt, rather than a deed accomplished.'

John Keats, Preface to *Endymion*

✻

John Osborne on ballet: 'poofs' football'.

✻

'[The Queen] is the only member of the Royal Family who is not an embarrassment in some way or another. As to . . . giving the Prince of Wales something to do . . . he would be fitted for about any form of employment better than he would be fitted to be King of England . . . If such a tactless, cranky, bad-tempered figure was to ascend the throne at this juncture – to say nothing of his rocky relations with his wife – it would only be a matter of time before we all decided that it was time to declare a Republic.'

A. N. Wilson, *Spectator*

✻

From an article by Paul Theroux on Graham Greene:

'He did not regard madness as a weakness or a moral fault, it was another way of seeing the world, another form of inspiration. "Much Madness is divinest Sense."'

The New York Times

'How can I know what I think until I hear what I say?'
Edward Garnett

'How can I tell what I feel until I see what I do?'
Constance Garnett

✳

'His eye ambitious, his gait majestical, and his general behaviour vain, ridiculous, and thrasonical.'
William Shakespeare, *Love's Labours Lost*

✳

Life is like a Tibetan prayer-wheel: give it a whirl.

✳

'It is like a barber's chair that fits all buttocks, the pin-buttock, the quatch-buttock, the brawn-buttock or any buttock.'
William Shakespeare, *All's Well that Ends Well*

✳

St Augustine was asked where time came from. He replied:

'Time comes from the future, which does not yet exist, into the present, which has no duration, and goes into the past, which has ceased to exist.'

'All our goodness is a loan; God is the owner.
God works and His work is God.'

St John of the Cross

✻

Mrs Richardson heard on BBC radio:
'You have been listening to *Prélude à l'après-midi d'un phone.*'

✻

"It'll be the best in the long run."
'"I'm sometimes happy when I think I shan't live to
see the long run."'

Anthony Trollope, *The Prime Minister*

✻

'Tis not the time, 'tis not the sophists vex him;
There is some root of suffering in himself,
Some secret and unfollow'd vein of woe,
Which makes the time look black and sad to him.'

Matthew Arnold, 'Empedocles on Etna'

✻

Yesterday, in NatWest in St James's St, a very tall aristo-
cratic-looking man of about my age cashing a cheque: 'I'd
like two fives and a ten, if you would be so kind,' he said into
the grille. His right shoulder was much larger than his left
and dropped away at an alarming angle. He wore a light
tweed overcoat — it was a warm day — and a very expensive-
looking black felt hat with a brim which had been steamed

to various eccentric curlings. 'Oh, thank you so much!' he
said when he'd been given the money. 'Too kind! Too kind.'

❋

'No, when the fights begins within himself,
A man's worth something.'
          Robert Browning, 'Bishop Blougram's Apology'

❋

Overheard: an American couple leaving a London theatre
after seeing Uncle Vanya. *One turned to the other and said:*
'I didn't like it as much as The Cherry Sisters.*'*
          (Told by Jill Balcon)

❋

Misty morning. Large spider web, looking like ghostly sails
of yachts, spread all around in Bonsai trees; the spindle tree,
which for a week has been a brilliant crimson, now appears to
be dusted down. All very beautiful.

❋

'I was no tree walking.
I was still. They ignored me,
the birds, the migrants
on their way south. They re-leafed
the trees, budding them
with their notes. They filtered through
the boughs like sunlight,
looked at me from three feet

off, their eyes blackberry bright,
not seeing me, not detaching me
from the withies, where I was
caged and they free.'

      R. S. Thomas, 'A Thicket in Lleyn'

    ✷

'The Whartons were very much moved. They were in a
state of enthusiasm at these news, amounting almost to
fury.'

      Anthony Trollope, *The Prime Minister*

    ✷

*On reflection, it seems an impertinence, when toddling on
towards eighty, to associate with people a lot younger, feeling
one can interest or entertain them. Well, not 'can' but possibly 'could'.*

    ✷

'I didn't feel she was interested at all in Harry's enthusiastic breakdown of my career or the promise of any
future if indeed she was listening. However she smiled a
kind of dreamy encouragement across at me.'

      John Osborne, *Almost a Gentleman*

*Am enjoying the Osborne book. Said to Alan Bennett today
of it: 'He doesn't even hiss like a snake but strikes straight
away.' Alan said it would be a good endorsement or blurb on
the book's cover.*

Lindsay Anderson sent his script of The Cherry Orchard *to some film-funding company. He received a letter back saying, 'Dear Mr Chekhov, We regret we do not think your story* The Cherry Orchard *is very suitable material.' Or words to that effect.*

✷

The light at sunset yesterday evening wasn't exactly lurid but was a disturbing mauve, and at 8 a.m. this morning it was a curious grey-yellow. For a couple of weeks now I have entertained a nightmarish image that the Gates of Hell, always ajar in our times, were creakingly opening wider.

✷

Apart from the depression of the sales, the number of closed shops, shifting landmarks and dangerously uneven pavements, London seems to have a new malaise: the proliferation of 'reject china' shops.

✷

'As is well known, literature ceases to be literature when it commits itself to moral uplift; it becomes moral philosophy or some such dull thing.'
    Anthony Burgess, *The Kingdom of the Wicked*

FITTON: 'But what if Spinola have a new project:
    To bring an army over in cork shoes
    And land them here at Harwich? All his horse
    Are shod with cork, and fourscore pieces of ordnance,
    Mounted upon cork carriages, with bladders
    Instead of wheels, to run the passage over
    At a spring tide.'
PENNYBOY JUNIOR: 'Is't true?'
FITTON: 'As true as the rest . . .'
NATHANIEL: 'They write from Leipzig (reverence to
        your ears)
    The art of drawing farts out of dead bodies
    Is by the Brotherhood of the Rosy Cross
    Produc'd unto perfection . . .'

Also, from the same play:

'Ha' you any news from the Indies? Any miracle
Done in Japan by the Jesuits? or in China?'

    Ben Jonson, *The Staple of News*

        ✳

'There was a young lady of Ryde
Who went in and out with the tide.
    When her friends said "stop clowning –
    Are you waving or drowning"
She admitted, "I can't quite decide."'

    Roger Woddis, *Spectator*

'There was a young lady of Norway,
Who crawled on all fours through a doorway.
    When someone asked why,
    She simply said, "I
do it my way and *you* do it your way."'
    Noel Petty, *Spectator*

✳

Watched final instalment of Churchill TV programme; gripping and moving. How well, as a nation, we do big-occasion funerals. (That was last night. Today there is an 'outrage' kiss-in planned to take place outside Parliament, and 'gay' soliciting in Piccadilly. Oh dear. No comment.)

✳

Titles?
A Halcyon Day
The Halcyon Days

✳

Dido's bark is like a penny whistle.

✳

'It was the Americans, not the English oddly enough,
who invented *keep a stiff upper lip* (1815), plus *fly off the
handle* (1825), *get religion* (1826) . . . *in cahoots* (1829) . . .
barking up the wrong tree (1833), plus . . . [in the] 1820s . . .
get the hang of a thing and . . . *there's no two ways about it.*'
    Paul Johnson, *The Birth of the Modern*

Sidney Lee, of Edward VII's gluttony:
'He had a splendid appetite and seldom toyed with his food.'

❊

'All the Christian virtues rolled into one make a ball that won't bounce.'

Nigel Nicolson, *Spectator*

❊

Last night watched TV film by Robert Gardner called Forest of Bliss — *largely about the burning ghats of Benares. Very striking and compelling and visually fine, as if Whistler had been let loose on the Ganges. The most rewarding thing about it was there was no commentary or music — just the natural sounds around the camera.*

❊

She was the sort of woman who was eager to be the first to pass on bad news and she was greatly rattled if she found she had been forestalled.

❊

'We can hardly be confident of the state of our own minds, but as it stands attested by some external action; we are seldom sure that we sincerely meant what we omitted to do.'

Dr Johnson, letter to Hester Thrale, 20 July 1775

'We all live on this condition that the ties of every endearment must at last be broken.'

Dr Johnson, letter to Mary Cholmondeley, 6 May 1777

'On Sunday Mr Green paid a visit from Lichfield, and, having nothing to say, said nothing and went away.'

Dr Johnson, 12 July 1775

٭

'A judge in De Funiak Springs, Florida, ordered that an inscription of the Ten Commandments on a courthouse wall must be covered during a murder trial, after the defence lawyer argued that the words "Thou Shalt Not Kill" might deprive jurors of their freedom of conscience.'

Daily Telegraph

٭

If there are 'born-again' Buddhists could it be said of them that they are 'born-again, born-again and born-again'?

Sea Calm

How still,
How strangely still
The water is today.
It is not good
For water
To be so still that way.

Langston Hughes

❋

I don't understand how blackbirds remain airborne when they skim so evenly only about ten inches over the ground.

Dreamed of a 'vanishing sea'. Something to do with a doubt-
ful phenomenon seen — if seen — from Beachy Head one hot
and hazy Sunday afternoon in about 1930. The tide appeared
to be in, then within minutes far out, and then — in a short
time — in again. We were on a school walk. It was com-
mented on at the time but nothing was reported in the papers.
I suppose this came into my mind because of a reading from
the Apocalypse at Mass about the 'seas drying up'.

✻

A dream last night in which a camp little old man talked on
and on, very boringly, at some conference. Roy Jenkins
(why?) said to me, 'Who is that awful creep?' and I replied,
'He's the lethal weapon in a snuff movie.' Madness.

✻

'Let this child say,
I hear the night bird, I can go to sleep.'
    C. Day Lewis, 'Last Words'

✻

'I think it was to Mrs Hamilton that [Lord] Jeffrey said in
allusion to the good taste of never losing the feminine in
the literary character, that there was no objection to the
blue stocking, provided the petticoat came low enough
down.'
    Henry Cockburn, *Memorials of His Time*

'Who hateth me but for my happiness?
Or who is honoured now but for his wealth?'
　　　Christopher Marlowe, *The Jew of Malta*

✷

Yesterday evening, on Channel 4, an excellent and charming Irish priest, very comically dressed, talked about Holy Communion always healing the 'fragmented' soul.

✷

Amos, the character I am to play (if we do the film) in Veterans *or* The Action Man. *I am beginning to note childish or slightly deranged behaviour in people, which could be of use to me. Yesterday evening at Mass a youth of about nineteen pulled the sleeve of his pullover down over his left wrist and sat sucking it.*

　　Into my memory, from somewhere, comes a boy constantly pulling up his left sock — unnecessarily.

✷

On our return from church:
Lapsed Catholic: 'Have a nice Mass?'
Self wanted to reply: 'Oh, you know; the same old thing. The Real Presence at the altar, body, blood, soul, divinity of Christ, as usual.'

'Answering to their names,
Out of the soil the buds come,
The silent detonations
Of power wielded without sin.'

> R. S. Thomas, 'The Garden'

✿

'Their rupture had resounded, and after being perfectly insignificant together they would be decidedly striking apart.'

> Henry James, *What Maisie Knew*

✿

'I, on men's impious uproar hurl'd,
Think often, as I hear them rave,
That peace has left the upper world
And now keeps only in the grave.'

> Matthew Arnold, 'Lines Written in Kensington Gardens'

✿

'In the public interest' — the phrase appears almost daily now and as often as not about subjects which only make interesting gossip. What would it sound like, as a claim for publishing, if 'neighbour' was substituted for 'public'? It is 'in the neighbours' interest' that they should know the woman opposite has taken a young man as lodger and her lights go out earlier than they used to.

If asked to write a few words about Barry Humphries's autobiography, More Please, *I might start:* 'Sandy Stone might say, *"Look, it's a thoroughly enjoyable read, but for a number of words I require Chambers Dictionary. For instance: erethism, caprine, lucifugous, geodesic, hireine, durian, reasty, hispid."* '

✻

Mountain Wizard

This figure of a mountain wizard
Carries both furs and fan
As if to show that timelessness
Began where time began.
Summer is winter, winter summer.
Ah, what a knowing man.

> Kakinomoto no Hitomaro, translated from the
> Japanese by Graeme Wilson

✻

There is an ad — for tourist accommodation to be opened shortly at Hampton Court. How long before we can get a room at Buck House?

✻

I have appeared in only two plays in the West End in the past fifteen years.

Miffed by hearing Melvyn Bragg on Radio 4 this morning
implying my comment on the West End Theatre was snob-
bish. I thought, meanly, if asked about him I'd say, 'one of
our better second-class novelists'.

On the same subject:
A ripple in a doll-sized teacup blown up into a media storm.

✳

A further madness – a letter from Mrs Lucy Pringle, inviting
me to lecture on corn circles. And yet more dottiness –
BAFTA is promoting awards for the best performances given
by actors in commercials.

✳

From the Daily Telegraph *Television and Radio Sup-*
plement, comment by Peter Read on Catholics and Sex,
Channel 4:

'Given Christ's forgiving attitude to the woman caught in
adultery, it's odd that the Roman Catholic Church should
have such a problem with sex. Tonight's programme
looks at the church and marriage. The ideal of one sexual
partner for life and the indissolubility of marriage vows
place an impossible strain on Catholics and, presumably,
on the church as it ties itself up in knots over issues like
sex outside marriage and contraception . . .'

Who is tied in knots? Mr Read, it would appear.

The Wisdom of Jonathan Ross – the flashy TV personality
– on programme on USA:
'Why, even Solomon chopped a baby in half.'

*

Old and Cold

'Now King David was old and stricken in years; and they
covered him with clothes, but he gat no heat.'

    I Kings 1:1

*

'The Princess was in the habit of saying to her guests
when she met them a day or two before one of her parties: "You will come, won't you?" as though she felt a
great desire to talk to them. But since, on the contrary,
she had nothing to talk to them about, when they entered
her presence she contented herself, without rising, with
breaking off for an instant her vapid conversation with
the two highnesses and the Ambassadors and thanking
them with: "How good of you to come," not because she
thought that the guest had shown goodness by coming,
but to enhance her own; then, at once dropping him back
into the stream, she would add: "You will find M. de
Guermantes by the garden door," so that the guest
proceeded on his way and ceased to bother her. To some
indeed she said nothing, contenting herself with showing
them her admirable onyx eyes, as though they had

come solely to visit an exhibition of precious stones.'

Marcel Proust, *Sodom and Gomorrah*

✻

The all-male semi-nude show the Chippendales, known 'in the trade' as 'the Chippolatas'.

✻

James Joyce's advertisement for Anna Livia Plurabelle — *not used by Faber and Faber:*

'Buy a book in brown paper
From Faber and Faber
To see Annie Liffey trip, tumble and caper.
Sevensinns in her singthings,
Plurabelle on her prose,
Seashell egg music wayriver she flows.'

✻

'One of the first essentials of creative art is the habit of imagining the most familiar things as vividly as the most surprising.'

Donald Tovey

'There should be in the soul halls of space, avenues of leisure and high porticos of silence, where God walks.'
　　Jeremy Taylor

✳

Philip Toynbee, diary entry, the year before he died:
'Trees have the power to startle me more and more.'

'I sometimes look at the knot in a piece of wood until I am frightened at it.'
　　William Blake

✳

On Christ:
'He had Eternity with him in the day that is called today, hence the next day had no power over him, it had no existence for him.'
　　Kierkegaard, *Christian Discourses*

✳

'When we come to have grey heads, and weak hands, moist eyes, and shrunk members.'
　　Ben Jonson, *The Silent Woman*

✳

'A small fire, the size of a cat, purred in the fireplace.'
　　John Updike, *Memories of the Ford Administration*

Shakespeare's Baby Talk

ELINOR: 'Come to thy grandam, child.'
CONSTANCE: 'Do, child, go to it grandam, child;
   Give grandam kingdom, and it grandam will
   Give it a plum, a cherry, and a fig.
   There's a good grandam.'
   King John

FOOL: 'For you know, nuncle,

   The hedge-sparrow fed the cuckoo so long,
   That it had it head bit off by it young.

   So out went the candle, and we were left darkling.'
   King Lear

＊

On eve of my eightieth year. The old must cease to boast of how old they are. God knows their age is apparent to everyone else.

＊

After this year's Oscar ceremonies in LA the young Irish (?) transvestite who was up for one was asked what he'd really like. He replied, 'Richard Gere. Right now. Here. Lying on the floor at my feet. Naked.'

'She was remarkably perceptive of human shortcomings.'
Kenneth Clark on Cynthia Nolan, Sidney Nolan's first wife

✻

US Press Headlines:

'Headless Man Found in Topless Bar.'
'Firemen Fight Fires in Piles of Tires.'
'Worthwhile Canadian Initiative', which, as one wag
put it, 'is not only boring as a whole, but boring
word by word'.

✻

'Thou hast set my feet in a large room.'
Psalm 31:8

✻

'A message from God
delivered by a bird
at my window, offering friendship.
Listen. Such language!
Who said God was without
speech? Every word an injection
to make me smile.'
R. S. Thomas, 'The Message'

'I don't like Miss Stackpole – everything about her displeases me; she talks so much too loud and looks at one as if one wanted to look at *her* – which one doesn't.'
Henry James, *The Portrait of a Lady*

✳

Margaret Beckett, Deputy Leader of the Labour Party:

'The debts are not tablets of stone handed down from Mount Olympus – or whatever.'

Mount Sinai, perhaps?

✳

From interview with Cis Berry (voice director with the Royal Shakespeare Company) by Robert Gore-Langton:

'Any criticism of somebody's voice is a criticism of themselves as well. The whole thing about correcting accents in schools is in my view quite criminal. We should never iron out accents.' And: 'After the opening of *Murder in the Cathedral* people said to me, "Wasn't it wonderful, it was so clear." That really pissed me off. Clarity is important, but they shouldn't like something simply because they can hear and digest it easily.'

'O wanderer from a Grecian shore,
Still, after many years in distant lands,
Still nourishing in thy bewilder'd brain
That wild, unquench'd, deep-sunken, old-world pain –
Say, will it never heal?'
    Matthew Arnold, 'Philomela'

✢

'No spring, nor summer beauty hath such grace
As I have seen in one autumnal face.'
    John Donne, 'Elegy IX'

✢

'For the night is already at hand, and it is well to yield to
the night.'
    Homer, *The Iliad*

✢

'The barking of the Sphinx.'
    R. L. Stevenson

✢

'The narrow mind is the discontented one.
There is pleasure in wisdom, there is wisdom in pleasure.
If thou findest no honey in thy cake,
Put thy cake into honey with thine own right hand
Nor think it defiled thereby.'
    Walter Savage Landor

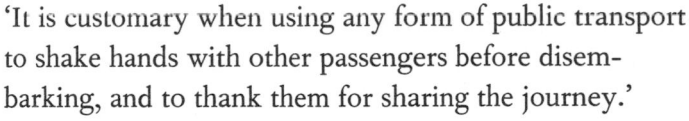

A competition in The Times, *some time ago, for the unkind-est advice to give to a tourist. The winning advice was:*

'It is customary when using any form of public transport to shake hands with other passengers before disembarking, and to thank them for sharing the journey.'

Dorothy Parker was asked by a friend how to put down a seriously ill cat. She answered, 'Try curiosity.'

✳

A well-known piece of literature retold in the metre of Hiawatha:

'You shall hear how Lady Constance,
Tiring of her wounded husband
(Poor Sir Clifford, high war-hero,
Inconvenienced by shrapnel),
Found a gamekeeper called Mellors
Who would teach her in his lunch-hour
(And in language frank and fearless
Such as wives and servants blush at)
To admire the lower orders.
While that blighted Bart, Sir Clifford
(Let us waste no pity on him,
For the man was paraplegic),
In his new electric wheelchair
Tried to drive it up a tunock –
Tried and tried, and couldn't make it.'

> Martin Woodhead

✳

An Australian vet to Googie Withers:
'You should talk to an animal every day for the good of your soul.'

'Sail not as if in pleasure boats upon a troubled sea.'
  Cardinal Newman

✷

*Recently I have noticed that the soles of my feet have become
scratchily lined as if with ancient runes.*

✷

'Set justice aside, and what are kingdoms but great bands
of brigands?'
  Cardinal Newman, echoing Augustine

'Earthly kingdoms are founded, not in justice but injustice.
They are created by the sword, by robbery, perjury, craft and
fraud. There never was a kingdom, except Christ's, which
was not conceived and born, nurtured and educated, in sin.'
  Cardinal Newman, but almost identical to Gregory VII's
  denunciation of Emperor Henry IV in 1080
  Quoted by David Newman in *The Two Cardinals*

✷

Abraham Constable (younger brother of John): 'When I
look at a mill painted by John I see that it will go *round.*'
John Constable: 'The sound of water escaping from mill-
dams etc., willows, old rotten planks, slimy posts, and
brickwork, I love such things . . . As long as I do paint, I
shall never cease to paint such places.'
  Quoted by Paul Johnson in *The Birth of the Modern*

'The proud Parnassian sneer,
The conscious simper, and the jealous leer,
Mix on his look.'

Alexander Pope, *Dunciad*

✳

'When the Ideal is manifested in the work-a-day world, it does
not put to shame the creatures of a day – it brings them nearer
to itself. Thus, when Homer causes Pegasus, a mortal thorough-
bred, to be put in as an outrigger with the divine horses of
Achilles, he is careful to tell us that Pegasus, though he "was
only an ordinary horse", kept up with the immortal pair.'

E. V. Rieu, Introduction to *The Iliad*

✳

'I'm not afraid to die. I just don't want to be around when
it happens.'

Woody Allen

✳

From the Sunday Telegraph, *'Me and My God' column:*

'In a world destroying itself by over-population the Pope
is making it worse. Love expressed in sex is one of the
few things everybody can afford. But for him it is a sin. It
was a great mistake to make an ignorant Polish peasant
into a Pope.'

The Rev. Chad Varah, rector of St Stephen Walbrook,
City of London

Last night woke from sleep about 2.30 a.m., thinking of Firs in the party scene [in The Cherry Orchard*]. I said to myself I must tell Lindsay Anderson that I think it important Firs should sit down for a bit during the dancing – a) he is not very well; b) he disapproves of the guests. This morning I telephoned Mander and Mitchenson in Beckenham, asking if they had any photographs of Firs in the 1958 Moscow Art Theatre production and, even more importantly, in the 1904 Stanislavsky production. They got back to me within an hour to say 'yes'. A photo of Rinbou(?) in 1958, and one of the party scene in 1904. 'You can pick out Firs in it,' they said, 'but it's not awfully clear because he's* sitting down*.' Odd.*

103

From LAMDA leaflet on forthcoming production of The Cherry Orchard:

'The dying Chekhov appears to contemplate a world in which humanity is exhausted, reduced to a futile pattern of physical gestures, squeaky boots, pratfalls, conversations with bookcases or with the setting sun. Here the absence of humanity can seem a consummation devoutly to be wished.'

Nick Worral

✴

Some ghastly 'comedienne' at the televised comedy awards last Sunday referred to Margaret Rutherford as having a face like an 'arse-hole'. And the audience laughed. Oh dear.

✴

Age withered her and custom staled her lack of variety.

✴

Note, of a Bacon portrait: 'He wasn't exactly an oil painting.'

My Boy Jack

'Have you news of my boy Jack?'
  Not this tide.
'When d'you think that he'll come back?'
  Not with this wind blowing, and this tide.

'Has any one else had word of him?'
  Not this tide.
For what is sunk will hardly swim,
  Not with this wind blowing, and this tide.

'Oh, dear, what comfort can I find?'
  None this tide,
  Nor any tide,
Except he did not shame his kind —
  Not even with that wind blowing, and that tide.

Then hold your head up all the more,
  This tide,
  And every tide;
Because he was the son you bore,
  And gave to that wind blowing and that tide!

  Rudyard Kipling

  ✵

A popcorn dispenser in the foyer at the Albery Theatre. Old Bronson Albery must be 'bursting his cerements'.

'The distinction between past, present and future is only an illusion, however persistent.'
  Albert Einstein

✻

'I suppose there are few friendships which can stand the test of correspondence.'
  Ernest Dowson

✻

'My dwelling is plucked up and removed from me like a shepherd's tent; like a weaver I have rolled up my life; he cuts me off from the loom.'
  Isaiah 38:12

✻

The point of a knighthood for British actors is to enable them to play butlers.

✻

'Cause me to hear thy lovingkindness in the morning.'
  Psalm 143:8

✻

'Here is the body pent,
Absent from Him I roam,
Yet nightly pitch my moving tent
A day's march nearer home.'
  James Montgomery, 'At Home in Heaven'

David Lean told me, in Ceylon, that swimming in the river
one evening he came face to face with a cobra swimming in
the opposite direction. They both turned and fled. I should
have commented, 'Wise cobra!'

✳

'Not so in love this mortal morning –
The finally unimportant dead,
Wish now no headline left to shed.
His useless life a useful warning.
Take as always the wrong turning
And bothers me with thoughts of God.'
Quentin Stevenson

✳

'Thus saith the Lords of hosts, the God of Israel, Amend
your ways and your doings, and I will cause you to dwell
in this place.

'Trust ye not in lying words, saying, The temple of the
Lord, The temple of the Lord . . .'
Jeremiah 7:3–4

✳

An odd, half-dreamed sentence came to me today:
'Mr and Mrs – didn't laugh at the same things; in fact they
seldom laughed except daily, and at someone else's expense,
but they were certainly scandalized by the same things.'

'When Housman died Cyril Connolly deprecated his inflated reputation. The heavens opened. Late for the funeral, Mr Connolly at least had the satisfaction of arriving in time to spit upon the grave before the mourners departed.'

> John Sparrow, quoted by Noel Annan in *Our Age*

❋

'And silence sounds no worse than cheers
After earth has stopped the ears.'

> A. E. Housman, 'To an Athlete Dying Young',
> *A Shropshire Lad*

❋

The steady, direct look of the congenital liar, thief and dipsomaniac.

❋

Norman Lamont's mouth like the neck of a party balloon.

❋

'Imaginary evil is romantic and varied; real evil is gloomy, monotonous, barren, boring. Imaginary good is boring; real good is always new, marvellous, intoxicating. "Imaginative literature", therefore, is either boring or immoral or a mixture of both.'

> Simone Weil

Best performance of the year:
Aston Villa v. *Milan, September 1994.*

❋

Dog names:
P. G. Wodehouse's dog – Wonder
Duke and Duchess of Windsor's cairn terrier – Pookey

❋

A fair share of 'diminutions' (Teilhard de Chardin's word).

❋

'Put thou my tears in thy bottle.'
   Psalm 56:8

'. . . give thy repose
To the wet sea-boy . . .'
William Shakespeare, 2 *Henry IV*

✻

*Lunched alone in Connaught Grill. At next table was a
middle-aged Hooray Henry, with a booming Estuary accent,
who was entertaining a Japanese businessman. 'If you want to
do business in England you must know some jokes. You know
– jokes. Like: A Scotchman and an Irishman and a Jew, and
so on. And shaggy-dog stories. You know what I mean by
shaggy dog?' 'Ah-so?' 'Yeah, well, that's another joke too –
about your Emperor.'*

✻

'On Monday I was standing by your bed, holding your
hand, small as the folded wing of a tiny bat, cold and
damp, your eyes sightless, blue, empty, moving gently to
the sound of my voice,' *etc., etc.*
From a letter to Kathleen Tynan by Dirk Bogarde, published in the *Daily Telegraph* after her death

✻

*Mrs Mary Leiter (wife of a Chicago mining tycoon), having
crossed the Atlantic for the first time: 'At last I am back on
terracotta.'*

✻

'A dungeon horrible, on all sides round
As one great furnace flamed, yet from those flames

No light, but rather darkness visible
Serv'd only to discover sights of woe,
Regions of sorrow, doleful shades, where peace
And rest can never dwell, hope never comes
That comes to all.'

    John Milton, *Paradise Lost*

✳

Do children still have jokey conundrums? I doubt it.
When is a door not a door? (When it's ajar.)
Why did the stamp stamp? (Because it saw the pillar box.)
Why did the fly fly? (Because the spider spied 'er.)

✳

'Where I saw, in Major Watson, such calm type of truth,
gentleness, and simplicity, as I have myself found in sol-
diers or sailors only; and so admirable to me that I have
never been able, since those Woolwich times, to gather
myself up against the national guilt of war, seeing that
such men were made by the discipline of it.'

    John Ruskin, *Praeterita*

✳

'It's a Boo –'

Then, silence. Some fancied they heard in the air
  A weary and wandering sigh
That sounded like "–jum!" but the others declare
  It was only a breeze that went by.'

    Lewis Carroll, *The Hunting of the Snark*

Strange ghostly dream of passing an attractive young woman
on the totally empty Marine Parade (Brighton) going towards
Black Rock. It was a beautiful, pale blue morning, sunny and a
little misty, not a breath of wind. The girl was coming towards
me, smiling to herself – but she was battling with a violent wind
– scarf flying, holding on to a cloche hat. It was a wind that
only touched her. For me, as I passed her, all was quiet.

✳

'Together with that pale, that white-fac'd shore,
Whose foot spurns back the ocean's roaring tides
And coops from other lands her islanders . . .'
    William Shakespeare, *King John*

✳

'And small birds fly in and out
  Of the world of man.'
    W. H. Auden, 'The Riddle'

✳

Psalm 46, King James Version:

> *Forty-sixth word from the top – shake*
> *Forty-sixth word from the bottom – speare*
> *Shakespeare's age in 1610, when the King James*
>   *Version is completed (publication 1611),*
> *is forty-six.*

LEPIDUS (*drunk*): '. . . I have heard the Ptolemies' pyramises are very goodly things; without contradiction I have heard that.'

SECOND GUARD: 'The star is fall'n.'
FIRST GUARD: 'And time is at his period.'

SOOTHSAYER: 'You shall outlive the lady whom you serve.'
CHARMIAN: 'O excellent! I love long life better than figs.'

William Shakespeare, *Antony and Cleopatra*

✳

'Little or nothing is to be expected from the shame of deferring what it is so wicked and perilous to defer. Profligacy in taking office is so extreme, that we have no doubt public men may be found, who, in half a century, would postpone all remedies for a pestilence, if the preservation of their places depended upon the propagation of the virus.'

Sydney Smith, 'Catholics', *Edinburgh Review*

✳

'Cant is the voluntary overcharging or prolongation of a real sentiment; hypocrisy is the setting up a pretension to a feeling you never had and have no wish for.'

William Hazlitt

'One's country has no right to demand everything. There is much that is higher and better and greater than one's country. One is patriotic only because one is too small and weak to be cosmopolitan.'

Anthony Trollope, letter to Kate Field, 1862

✷

From the Prologue to Edward Gordon Craig's book on Henry Irving:

'We all have plenty of material to embroider on, whoever we come to write about, but one needs the nature of a malicious valet or soured lady's maid to dream of doing so – and some of their vindictiveness, to do the thing quite brilliantly.'

✷

'What is the price of Experience? do men buy it for a
    song?
Or Wisdom for a dance in the street?'

William Blake, *The Four Zoas*

✷

        'Let thy West Wind sleep on
The lake; speak silence with thy glimmering eyes,
And wash the dusk with silver.'

William Blake, 'Thou Fair-Haired Angel of the Evening'

'Thou that art now the world's fresh ornament,
And only herald to the gaudy spring.'
    William Shakespeare, 'Sonnet I'

    ✻

'The stars are not wanted now: put out every one;
Pack up the moon and dismantle the sun;
Pour away the oceans and sweep up the wood;
For nothing now can ever come to any good.'
    W. H. Auden, 'IX', *Twelve Songs* ('Stop all the clocks')

    ✻

'Sentimentality, the ostentatious parading of excessive and
spurious emotion, is the mark of dishonesty, the inability
to feel; the wet eyes of the sentimentalist betray his aver-
sion to experience, his fear of life, his arid heart; and it is
always, therefore, the signal of secret and violent inhu-
manity, the mask of cruelty.'
    James Baldwin, *Notes of a Native Son*

    ✻

'The lines are fallen unto me in pleasant places.'
    Psalm 16:6

    ✻

'Behold, I have graven thee upon the palms of my
hands . . .'
    Isaiah 49:16

Would it be fair to say of John G., 'He is a great actor and his own most appreciative audience'?

✴

'Every artist works, like the Gobelin weavers, on the wrong side of the tapestry, and if now and then he comes round to the right side, and catches what seems a happy glow of colour and a firm sweep of design, he must instantly retreat again.'
Edith Wharton

✴

'Every morning I introduce myself to myself, and every night I tell myself that we have had a delightful day together, but the acquaintanceship remains experimental.'
Max Beerbohm

✴

'I totter a little but make a shift to walk.'
Jonathan Swift

✴

'She bears the purse too; she is a region in Guiana, all gold and bounty.'
William Shakespeare, *The Merry Wives of Windsor*

✴

'That nod unto the World'
William Shakespeare, *Antony and Cleopatra*

'Forsake thy cage,
    Thy rope of sands
Which petty thoughts have made.'
    George Herbert, 'The Collar'

✳

'It has been the peculiarity and the marvel of his power that he invested his puppets with a charm that has enabled him to dispense with human nature.'
    Anthony Trollope on Dickens, quoted by Albert H.
    Gordon at Annual US Trollope Society Dinner

✳

Compare to Lady Macbeth:

'The bastard brains with these my proper hands
Shall I dash out.'
    William Shakespeare, *The Winter's Tale*

✳

'The ultimate in gracious living: from the excellence of the food and wine, to the splendour of the period suites; house, hosts and staff ensure that the visitor feels truly at home.'
    Brochure for Kingston House, Devon

Not my home.

'. . . and like empty clouds
In which our faulty apprehensions forge
The forms of dragons, lions, elephants,
When they hold no proportion . . .'
George Chapman, *Bussy D'Ambois*

✳

Two lines added to Hamlet, *Act III Scene 2:*

HAMLET: 'Do you see yonder cloud that's almost in
  shape of a camel?'
POLONIUS: 'By the mass, and 'tis like a camel indeed.'
HAMLET: 'Methinks it is like a weasel.'
POLONIUS: 'It is backed like a weasel.'
HAMLET: 'Or like a whale?'
POLONIUS: 'Very like a whale.'

HAMLET: Perchance it is a UFO.
POLONIUS: My lord, it *is* a UFO.

'And the yonge sonne
Hath in the Ram his half cours yronne
And smale foweles maken melodye,
That slepen al the nyght with open ye
(So priketh hem nature in hir corages),
Thanne longen fok to goon on pilgrimages . . .'
Geoffrey Chaucer, Prologue, The Canterbury Tales

❋

Enter Hamlet, a footman, in haste
HAMLET: 'What, coachman! My lady's coach, for shame!
   Her Ladyship's ready to come down.'
Enter Potkin, a tankard bearer
POTKIN: "sfoot, Hamlet, are you mad?'

Then:
GERTRUDE (*sings*): 'His head as white as milk,
All flaxen was his hair;
But now he is dead
And laid in his bed,
And never will come again
God be at your labour!'
Ben Jonson et al, Eastward Ho!

Compare to Hamlet:
OPHELIA: 'And will he not come again?
And will he not come again?
   No no, he is dead,
   Go to thy death-bed,
He never will come again.

His head was white as snow,
All flaxen was his poll . . .
. . . God ha' mercy on his soul.'

✻

'Be ashamed . . . of leaning your elbow on the table.'
Ecclesiasticus 41:19

✻

'And he took the blind man by the hand, and led him out
of the town; and when he had spit on his eyes, and put his
hands upon him, he asked him if he saw ought.

'And he looked up, and said, I see men as trees, walking.

'After that he put his hands again upon his eyes, and
made him look up: and he was restored, and saw every
man clearly.'
Mark 8:23–25

✻

'You would be another Penelope; yet, they say, all the
yarn
She spun in Ulysses' absence did but fill Ithaca full of
moths.'
William Shakespeare, *Coriolanus*

From Meetings with Remarkable Trees *by Thomas Paken-
ham, about two great trees on the shores of Lough Erne,
County Fermanagh:*

'I showed the photograph to a camper whose brightly
coloured tent had been pitched just beyond the dark green
circle of branches. "What do you think of it?" I asked.
"Amazing," she replied. "Where is it? Far from here? I'd
like to see that." "Twenty feet away." '

❊

*The two small black sheep in the little paddock have eyes that
look like Glacier Mints stuck on the outside of their heads.*

❊

'When I love you, what do I love? It is not physical beauty
nor temporal glory nor the brightness of light dear to
earthly eyes, nor the sweet melodies of all kinds of songs,
nor the gentle odour of flowers and ointments and per-
fumes, nor manna or honey, nor limbs welcoming the
embraces of the flesh; it is not these I love when I love my
God. Yet there is a light I love, and a food, and a kind of
embrace when I love my God – a light, voice, odour, food,
embrace of my inner man, where my soul is floodlit by light
which space cannot contain, where there is sound that time
cannot seize, where there is a perfume which no breeze dis-
perses, where there is a taste for food no amount of eating
can lessen, and where there is a bond of union that no sat-
iety can part. That is what I love when I love my God.'

'Late have I loved you, beauty so old and so new.'
    St Augustine, *Confessions*

⁕

An autobiographical title?
'Dust in sunlight and memory in corners
Wait for the wind that chills towards the dead land.'
    T. S. Eliot, 'A Song for Simeon'

⁕

Title:
It Goes without Saying

⁕

'"She never loved him [Sebastian], you know, as we do."
  '"Do". The word reproached me; there was no past
tense in Cordelia's verb "to love".'
    Evelyn Waugh, *Brideshead Revisited*

⁕

*A radio conversation released by the Chief of US Naval Oper-
ations, October 1995:*

CANADIANS: 'Please divert your course fifteen degrees
    south to avoid a collision.'
AMERICANS: 'Recommend you divert your course fifteen
    degrees north to avoid a collision.'
CANADIANS: 'Negative. You will have to divert your
    course fifteen degrees to the south to avoid a collision.'

AMERICANS: 'This is the captain of a US Navy ship. I
say again, divert YOUR course.'
CANADIANS: 'No. I say again, you divert YOUR course.'
AMERICANS: 'THIS IS THE AIRCRAFT CARRIER USS LIN-
COLN, THE SECOND-LARGEST SHIP IN THE UNITED
STATES' ATLANTIC FLEET. WE ARE ACCOMPANIED BY
A TASK FORCE OF THREE DESTROYERS, THREE
CRUISERS, AND NUMEROUS SUPPORT VESSELS. I
DEMAND THAT YOU CHANGE YOUR COURSE FIFTEEN
DEGREES NORTH. I SAY AGAIN, THAT IS ONE-FIVE
DEGREES NORTH, OR COUNTER-MEASURES WILL BE
UNDERTAKEN TO ENSURE THE SAFETY OF THIS SHIP.'
CANADIANS: 'This is a lighthouse. Your call.'

✳

'How easy dost thou take all England up!
From forth this morsel of dead royalty.'

'The tackle of my heart is crack'd and burn'd,
And all the shrouds wherewith my life should sail
Are turned to one thread, one little hair.'

William Shakespeare, *King John*

✳

*To National Gallery to see various paintings – Van Dyck,
Turner, and above all Rubens's* Samson and Delilah. *Sat in
front of it for ten minutes. Fascinated by the hard, dead skin
on sole of Samson's foot, the lightness of Delilah's touch
on his shoulder, and the typical Mr Teasy-Weasy who is*

snipping off his hair. It looks as if it's going to be a very chic hairdo. Alan B. says there is much controversy about whether it's by Rubens. But if not, by whom?

✳

The frontispiece of Ben Jonson's The New Inn:

The New Inn
or
The Light of Heart
A Comedy

As it was never acted, but most negligently
played by some, the King's servants, and more
squeamishly beheld, and censured, by others,
the King's subjects.
1629

✳

'But the iniquity of oblivion blindly scattereth her poppy.'
Sir Thomas Browne, *Hydriotaphia*

✳

'A newspaper that wishes to make its fortune should
never waste its columns and weary its readers by praising
anything. Eulogy is invariably dull.'
Anthony Trollope, *The Way We Live Now*

'Here I am, an old man in a dry month,
Being read to by a boy, waiting for rain.'
>   T. S. Eliot, 'Gerontion'

'April is the cruellest month, breeding
Lilacs out of the dead land, mixing
Memory and desire, stirring
Dull roots with spring rain.'
>   T. S. Eliot, 'Burial of the Dead', *The Waste Land*

✴

Thomas Beecham to a player in his orchestra:
'We cannot expect you to be with us all the time, but perhaps
you would be good enough to keep in touch now and then.'

✴

'Dom Sebastian Moore of Downside Abbey maintains
that his life of contemplative prayer began when he had
the honesty to tell the Lord: "You bore me."'
>   Quoted by Dame Philippa Edwards, *The Tablet*

✴

From Quentin Stevenson — quoting John Ruskin:

'It is not cheaper things
We want to possess,
But expensive things
That cost a lot less.'

'May He support us all the day long till the shades lengthen and the evening comes and the busy world is hushed and the fever of life is over and our work is done, then in His mercy may He give us a safe lodging and a holy rest and peace at the last.'

Cardinal Newman

✻

' "This is fairyland," said Lopez to the Duchess, as he left the room.

' "Come and be a fairy then," she answered, very graciously. "We are always on the wing about this hour on a Wednesday night." '

Anthony Trollope, *The Prime Minister*

✻

Advent, Week 1, Friday, the Divine Office
'Come now, insignificant man, fly for a moment from your affairs, escape for a little while from the tumult of your thoughts. Put aside now your weighty cares and leave your wearisome toils. Abandon yourself for a little to God and rest for a little in him.

'Enter into the inner chamber of your soul, shut out everything save God and what can be of help in your quest for him and having locked the door seek him out. Speak now, my whole heart, speak now to God: "I seek your countenance, O Lord, your countenance I seek." '

St Anselm, *Proslogion*

'I wants to make your flesh creep.'
      Charles Dickens, *The Pickwick Papers*, the fat boy

✷

'If you take faith away from the people you will end by producing nothing but highway robbers.'
      Napoleon

✷

From a letter of Fr John O'Connor to David Johns, 1921:
'The great miracles are too big to see and the small ones too numerous to count.'

✷

'Hermodorus the poet wrote verses in honour of Antigonus in which he called him Offspring of the Sun; he retorted, "The man who slops out my chamber-pot knows nothing about that!"'
      Montaigne, 'On the inequality there is between us', *Essays*

✷

'I should fear those that dance before me now
Would one day stamp upon me. It has been done:
Men shut their doors against a setting sun.'
      William Shakespeare, *Timon of Athens*

A bizarre dream

M and I gave a big lunch party in some smart hotel (not one I recognized) for the cast of whatever play I was in (unknown). About twenty people, but more and more kept arriving, many of whom I didn't know, and there was a seating problem. I kept saying, 'Lemen hasn't arrived yet. Late as usual', and someone whispered to me, 'Lemen is dead.' 'I know that,' I said, 'a lot of people here are also dead — Mick Balcon, Martita Hunt, and all the people sitting at the end of the table.'

'Today, characteristically, mourners like to personalize funerals, using the service as an occasion to eulogize their loved ones, and expunging, as far as they are able, mention of death itself. And so they are robbed of a most significant moment to set existence into a realistic context. We are given life as a gift; we leave the earth with an added value known only to God.'

Rev. Dr Denis Duncan

✳

'A young Apollo, golden-haired,
Stands dreaming on the verge of strife,
Magnificently unprepared
For the long littleness of life.'

Frances Cornford, about Rupert Brooke

✳

'Others abide our question. Thou art free.
We ask and ask: Thou smilest and art still.'

Matthew Arnold, 'Shakespeare'

✳

Of poetry:
'It is original, not in the paltry sense of being new, but in the deeper sense of being old; it is original in the sense that it deals with origins.'

G. K. Chesterton, on Robert Browning

'Gloria had been an old-style Episcopalian, resenting any tampering with Cranmer's prayer-book language and any evangelical or feel-good pollutions of the service, such as a homily at morning prayer or the passing of the peace at any service. Perdita had drifted from Unitarianism into Buddhism and settlement-house good works. Both women were religious aristocrats, for whom God was a vulgar poor relation with the additional social disadvantage of not existing.'

John Updike, *Toward the End of Time*

❋

Sir Hugh Casson, on a lady who married an English diplomat: 'Finally she settled for a furled umbrella.'

❋

'Time hath, my lord, a wallet at his back,
Wherein he puts alms for oblivion,
A great-siz'd monster of ingratitudes.'

William Shakespeare, *Troilus and Cressida*

❋

'It is a sad thing to see a man who has been frittered away piecemeal by petty distractions, and who has never done his best. But it is still sadder to see a man who has done his best, who has reached his utmost limits – and finds his work a failure, and himself far less than he had imagined himself.'

Matthew Arnold

131

'For the blessing of God upon the grass is in shades of
  Green visible to a nice observer as they light upon the
  surface of the earth.'
  Christopher Smart

✳

'In Eternity there is no distinction of tenses.'
  Sir Thomas Browne, *Religio Medici*

✳

'Cleere had the day bin from the dawne,
All chequerd was the Skye,
Thin clouds like Scarfs of Cobweb Lawne
Vayld Heaven's most glorious eye.
The Winde had no more strength than this,
That leasurely it blew,
To make one leafe the next to kisse,
That closely by it grew.'
  Michael Drayton, 'The Sixt Nimphall'

✳

FIRST GENTLEMAN: 'The news, Rogero?'
SECOND GENTLEMAN: 'Nothing but bonfires: the oracle
  is fulfilled.'
  William Shakespeare, *The Winter's Tale*

'From this church they led their brides,
    From this church themselves were led
Shoulder-high . . .'
    Edmund Blunden, 'Forefathers'

            ✴

'Stay with me, Ariel, while I pack, and with your first free act
    Delight my leaving; share my resigning thoughts
As you have served my revelling wishes: then, brave
        spirit,
    Ages to you of song and daring, and to me
Briefly Milan, then earth.'
    W. II. Auden, 'Prospero to Ariel', *The Sea and the Mirror*

            ✴

'The first day when he pitcheth downe his tentes,
White is their hew, and on his silver crest
A snowy Feather spangled white he beares,
To signify the mildnesse of his minde,
That, satiate with spoile, refuseth blood:
But when Aurora mounts the second time,
As red as scarlet is his furniture;
Then must his kindled wrath bee quencht with blood,
Not sparing any that can manage armes:
But, if these threats moove not submission,
Black are his collours, black Pavilion,
IIis speare, his shield, his horse, his armour, plumes,
And Jetty feathers menace death and hell,
Without respect of Sex, degree or age . . .'
    Christopher Marlowe, *Tamburlaine*

'When as a child I laughed and wept,
      Time crept.
When as a youth I waxed more bold,
      Time strolled.
When I became a full grown man,
      Time ran.
When older still I daily grew,
      Time flew.
Soon I shall find, in passing on,
      Time gone.
"O Christ! Wilt thou have saved me then?"
  Amen.'

      Lines found on an old clock in Chester Cathedral,
      by Canon Henry Twells

'I remember being present when he showed himself to be so corrupted, or at least something so different from what I think right, as to maintain, that a member of parliament should go along with his party, right or wrong . . . It is maintaining that you may lie to the public; for you lie when you call that right which you think wrong, or the reverse.'

Dr Johnson, quoted in Boswell's *Life of Dr Johnson*

'We Open in Venice'

A troupe of strolling players are we,
Not stars like L. B. Mayer's are we,
But just a simple band
Who roams about the land
Dispensing fol-de-rol frivolitee.
Mere folk who give distraction are we,
No Theatre Guild attraction are we,
But just a crazy group
That never ceases to troop
Around the map of little Italee.

We open in Venice
We next play Verona,
Then on to Cremona.
(Lotsa dough in Cremona.)
Our next jump is Parma.
(That dopey, mopey menace.)
Then Mantua, then Padua,
Then we open again,
Where?
In Venice.

Cole Porter, *Kiss Me Kate*

'A grieving mother was told to remove a cross from her son's grave because it represents "excessive use of the Christian symbol". The Lincolnshire diocese told Patricia Gearing that a Micky Mouse headstone would be more suitable.'

The Week

✳

'It is not our folly which makes me laugh: it is our wisdom.'

Montaigne, 'On three kinds of social intercourse', *Essays*

'The archer who shoots beyond his target misses it just as much as the one who falls short; my eyes trouble me as much when I suddenly come up into a strong light as when I plunge into darkness.'

Montaigne, 'On moderation', *Essays*

✳

'And there with moderate meate, and wine, and fire,
Have past the howres contentedly with chat,
Now talk'd of this, and then discours'd of that.'

Michael Drayton, 'To Henry Reynolds, of Poets and Poesie'

✳

'Unpack my heart with words . . .'

William Shakespeare, *Hamlet*

'It is reason and wisdom which takes away cares, not places affording wide views over the sea.'
      Horace, *Epistles*

*

'The girl beside him appealed, strangely, to his sense of character . . . satisfied that her quality would be very much her own, and neither borrowed nor reflected nor imposed.'
      Henry James, *Roderick Hudson*

*

                'O you heavenly charmers,
What things you make of us? For what we lack
We laugh, for what we have, are sorry still,
Are children in some kind. Let us be thankful
For that which is, and with you leave dispute
That are above our question. Let's go off,
And bear us like the time.'
      William Shakespeare, *The Two Noble Kinsmen*

*

'At Christmas I no more desire a rose
Than wish a snow in May's new fangled shows;
But like of each thing that in season grows.'

FERDINAND: 'Come, sir, it wants a twelvemonth and a
day,
And then 'twill end.'
BIRON: 'That's too long for a play.'

William Shakespeare, *Love's Labours Lost*

✳

'For truth itself is not privileged to be used all the time
and in all circumstances: noble though its employment is,
it has its limits and boundaries.'

Montaigne, 'On experience', *Essays*

✳

'I have seen all the deadly vices march in order across his
face and leave it washed and empty for the virtues.'

Said of Paul Verlaine, quoted by Quentin Stevenson

✳

'I have no Genius to disputes in Religion, and have often
thought it wisdom to decline them, especially upon a disadvantage, or when the causes of truth might suffer in the
weakness of my patronage.'

Sir Thomas Browne, *Religio Medici*

The Cockerel

The cockerel wakes his neighbours up
With rude red shouts.
He sings in scat
A rat-tat-tat
Magnificat.
He has no doubts.

Perched on a dunghill belting out
His hymn of praise,
He magnifies
And glorifies
The morning skies.
I like his ways.

Old cock, old crony, sing for me
Who cannot crow.
O chant it clear
So all can hear
Both far and near:
Co co rico
And *cock-a-doodle-doodle-do*.
Would I could pray as well as you!

Robert Nye

Finch

The finch, an inch or two of fire,
A feathered green Orfeo,
He bobs and throbs on the barbed wire,
Singing in sleet in May, oh!
He sings of all and everything
To do with his desire for Spring;
He sings because he has to sing:
In jubilate Deo.

Robert Nye

✳

'Sir —
I was at Silverstone on Sunday. Watching from Copse
Corner, I was revolted when large elements of the crowd,
mostly Damon Hill fans, cheered when they saw Michael
Schumacher crash. My first thought was that perhaps they
did not appreciate the potential for serious injury of an
accident at such high speed. However, there was then a
second cheer when the same people saw that he was
unable to get out of the car. This was completely inex-
cusable.'

Alastair Parker, letter to the *Daily Telegraph*

✳

Vernon Dobicheff of Caryl Brahms:
'She scuttled off like an important scarab.'

'I do not like curing one ill by another; I loathe remedies which are more importunate than the sickness: being subject to colic paroxysms and then made to abstain from the pleasure of eating oysters are two ills for the price of one. On this side we have the illness hurting us, on the other the diet. Since we must risk being wrong, let us risk what gives us pleasure, rather.'

Montaigne, 'On experience', *Essays*

✳

'There was a young maid of Torquay
Whose motions were not very free
　　So they gave her a mixture
　　Which kept her a fixture
For W-E-E-E-E-K S in the w.c.'

Patricia McNabb

✳

An Epitaph on Salathiel Pavy,
a Child of Queen Elizabeth's Chapel

Weep with me all you that read
　　This little story:
And know for whom a tear you shed,
　　Death's self is sorry.
'Twas a child that so did thrive
　　In grace, and feature,
As Heaven and Nature seemed to strive
　　Which owned the creature.

Years he numbered scarce thirteen
  When Fates turned cruel,
Yet three filled zodiacs had he been
  The stage's jewel;
And did act (what now we moan)
  Old men so duly,
As, sooth, the Parcae thought him one,
  He played so truly.
So, by error, to his fate
  They all consented;
But viewing him since (alas, too late)
  They have repented.
And have sought (to give new birth)
  In baths to steep him;
But, being so much too good for earth,
  Heaven vows to keep him.

Ben Jonson

✳

A spider's web, stretched between the uprights of the bird table, sagging with the weight of morning dew; the lawn looking like shattered glass glittering in the sun.

✳

'They despise pleasure but are rather weak in pain; they are indifferent to glory, but are broken by disgrace.'

Cicero, quoted by Montaigne

'No man ever was so free, when he was going to say a good thing, from a *look* that expressed that it was coming; or, when he had said it, from a look that expressed that it had come.'

> Dr Johnson on Mr Beauclerk, quoted by Boswell

✳

> 'But wouldst gabble like
A thing most brutish, I endow'd thy purposes
With words . . .'

> William Shakespeare, Prospero to Caliban, *The Tempest*

✳

'In short, Sir, I have got no further than this: every man has a right to utter what he thinks truth, and every other man has a right to knock him down for it. Martyrdom is the test.'

> Dr Johnson, quoted by Boswell

✳

'And the doors shall be shut in the streets, when the sound of the grinding is low, and he shall rise up at the voice of the bird, and all the daughters of music shall be brought low . . .

'Or ever the silver cord be loosed, or the golden bowl be broken, or the pitcher be broken at the fountain, or the wheel broken at the cistern.

'Then shall the dust return to the earth as it was: and the spirit shall return unto God who gave it.'
Ecclesiastes 12:4 and 6–7

✴

Half-awake dream in the night of a production of A Midsummer Night's Dream *in which Theseus and his court were all dressed in classical Greek style, Oberon, Titania and the fairies in Eliza-bethan costume, and the mechanicals in modern dress.*

✴

'The gimlet-eyed lady was fearless, formidable, eccentric, upper-class and athletic. She had a ten-acre voice.'
John le Carré, 'Sarratt and the Draper of Watford'

✴

'Thoughts, like old vultures, play upon their heart-strings.'
Isaac Watts

✴

'It made all the difference, in asserting any principle of war, whether one assumed that a discharge of artillery would merely knead down a certain quantity of once living clay into a level line, as in a brick-field; or whether, out of every separately Christian-named portion of the ruinous heap, there went out, into the smoke and dead-fallen air of battle, some astonished condition of soul, unwillingly released.'
John Ruskin, *The Crown of Wild Olive*

'And God gave Apollo
The Mind and the tongue
To speak the truth of God to mankind.
To open the future, to unriddle the present,
Where mankind huddles blindly, at a shut door.'

Aeschylus, *Eumenides*, translated by Ted Hughes

✳

'Pliny says each man is an excellent instruction unto himself provided he has the capacity to spy on himself from close quarter.'

Montaigne

'Just as some excellent clowns whom I have seen are able to give us all the delight which can be drawn from their art while wearing their everyday clothes, whereas to put

us in a laughing mood their apprentices and those who
are less deeply learned in that art have to put flour on
their faces, dress up in funny clothes and hide behind silly
movements and grimaces.'

    Montaigne, 'On books', *Essays*

✳

'Where there is no vision, the people perish.'

    Proverbs 29:18

✳

'For the bewitching of naughtiness doth obscure things
that are honest; and the wandering of concupiscence doth
undermine the simple mind.'

    Wisdom of Solomon 4:1

✳

'When he [Victor Hugo] took up residence in Guernsey,
his son asked him how he would spend his exile; he
replied that he would gaze at the ocean and asked his son
what he would do. "I," said the son, "I shall translate
Shakespeare." To which Hugo adds that the two activities
are one and the same.'

    Jonathan Bate, *The Genius of Shakespeare*

'Who hath gathered the wind in his fists? Who hath
bound the waters in a garment?'

Proverbs 30:4

✳

'By my troth I care not; a man can die but once: we
owe God a death: I'll ne'er bear a base mind:
an't be my destiny, so; an't be not, so: no man is
too good to serve's prince, and let it go which way
it will, he that dies this year is quit for the next.'

William Shakespeare, 2 *Henry IV*

'For I will consider my Cat Jeoffry.

For he is the servant of the Living God duly and daily serving him.

For at the first glance of the glory of God in the East he worships in his way.

For is this done by wreathing his body seven times round with elegant quickness.

For then he leaps up to catch the musk, which is the blessing of God upon his prayer.

For he rolls upon prank to work it in.

For having done duty and received blessing he begins to consider himself.

For this he performs in ten degrees.

For first he looks upon his fore-paws to see if they are clean.

For secondly he kicks up behind to clear away there.

For thirdly he works it upon stretch with the fore-paws extended.

For fourthly he sharpens his paws by wood.

For fifthly he washes himself.

For Sixthly he rolls upon wash.

For Seventhly he fleas himself, that he may not be interrupted upon the beat.

For Eighthly he rubs himself against a post.

For Ninthly he looks up for his instructions.

For Tenthly he goes in quest of food.

For having considered God and himself he will consider his neighbour.

For if he meets another cat he will kiss her in kindness.

For when he takes his pray he plays with it to give it a
  chance.
For one mouse in seven escapes by his dallying.
For when his day's work is done his business more
  properly begins.
For he keeps the Lord's watch in the night against the
  adversary.
For he counteracts the powers of darkness by his
  electrical skin and glaring eyes.
For he counteracts the Devil, who is death, by brisking
  about the life.
For in his morning orisons he loves the sun and the sun
  loves him.
For he is of the tribe of Tiger.
For the Cherub Cat is a term of the Angel Tiger.
For he has subtlety and hissing of a serpent, which in
  goodness he suppresses.
For he will not do destruction if he is well-fed, neither
  will he spit without provocation.
For he purrs in thankfulness, when God tells him he's a
  good Cat.
For he is an instrument for the children to learn
  benevolence upon.
For every house is incomplete without him and a blessing
  is lacking in the spirit.
For the Lord commanded Moses concerning the cats at
  the departure of the Children of Israel from Egypt.
For every family have one cat at least in the bag.
For the English Cats are best in Europe.

For he is the cleanest in the use of his fore-paws of any
    quadruped.
For the dexterity of his defence is an instance of the love
    of God to him exceedingly.
For he is the quickest to his mark of any creature.
For he is tenacious of his point.
For he is a mixture of gravity and waggery.
For he knows that God is his Saviour.
For there is nothing sweeter than his peace when at rest.
For there is nothing brisker than his life when in motion.
For he is of the Lord's poor and so indeed he is called by
    benevolence perpetually – Poor Jeoffry! Poor
    Jeoffry! the rat has bit thy throat.
For I bless the name of the Lord Jesus that Jeoffry is
    better.
For this divine spirit comes about his body to sustain it in
    complete cat.
For his tongue is exceeding pure so that it has in purity
    what it wants in music.
For he is docile and can learn certain things.
For he can set up with gravity which is patience upon
    approbation.
For he can fetch and carry, which is patience in
    employment.
For he can jump over stick which is patience upon proof
    positive.
For he can spraggle upon waggle at the word of
    command.
For he can jump from an eminence into his master's
    bosom.

For he can catch the cork and toss it again.
For he is hated by hypocrite and miser.
For the former is afraid of detection.
For the latter refuses the charge.
For he camels his back to bear the first notion of business.
For he is good to think on, if a man would express
    himself neatly.
For he made a great figure in Egypt for his signal
    services.
For he killed the Ichneumon-rat very pernicious by land.
For his ears are so acute that they sting again.
For from this proceed the passing quickness of his
    attention.
For by stroking of him I have found electricity.
For I perceived God's light about him both wax and fire.
For the Electrical fire is the spiritual substance, which
    God sends from heaven to sustain the bodies both of
    man and beast.
For God has blessed him in the variety of his movements.
For, tho' he cannot fly, he is an excellent clamberer.
For his motions upon the face of the earth are more than
    any other quadruped.
For he can tread to all the measures upon the music.
For he can swim for life.
For he can creep.'

    Christopher Smart, *Jubilate Agno*

'She had always understood that Fitz meant something aristocratic; there was Fitz-Roy – she thought that some of the King's children had been called Fitz-Roy; and there was Fitz-Clarence now – they were the children of dear good King William the Fourth. Fitz-Adam! – it was a pretty name; and she thought it very probably meant "Child of Adam". No one, who had not some good blood in their veins, would dare to be called Fitz; there was a deal in a name – she had had a cousin who spelt his name with two little ffs – ffoulkes – and he always looked down upon capital letters, and said they belonged to lately-invented families. She had been afraid he would die a batchelor, he was so very choice. When he met with a Mrs ffaringdon, at a watering-place, he took to her immediately; and a very pretty genteel woman she was – a widow with a very good fortune; and "my cousin", Mr ffoulkes, married her; and it was all owing to her two little ffs.'

Mrs Gaskell, *Cranford*

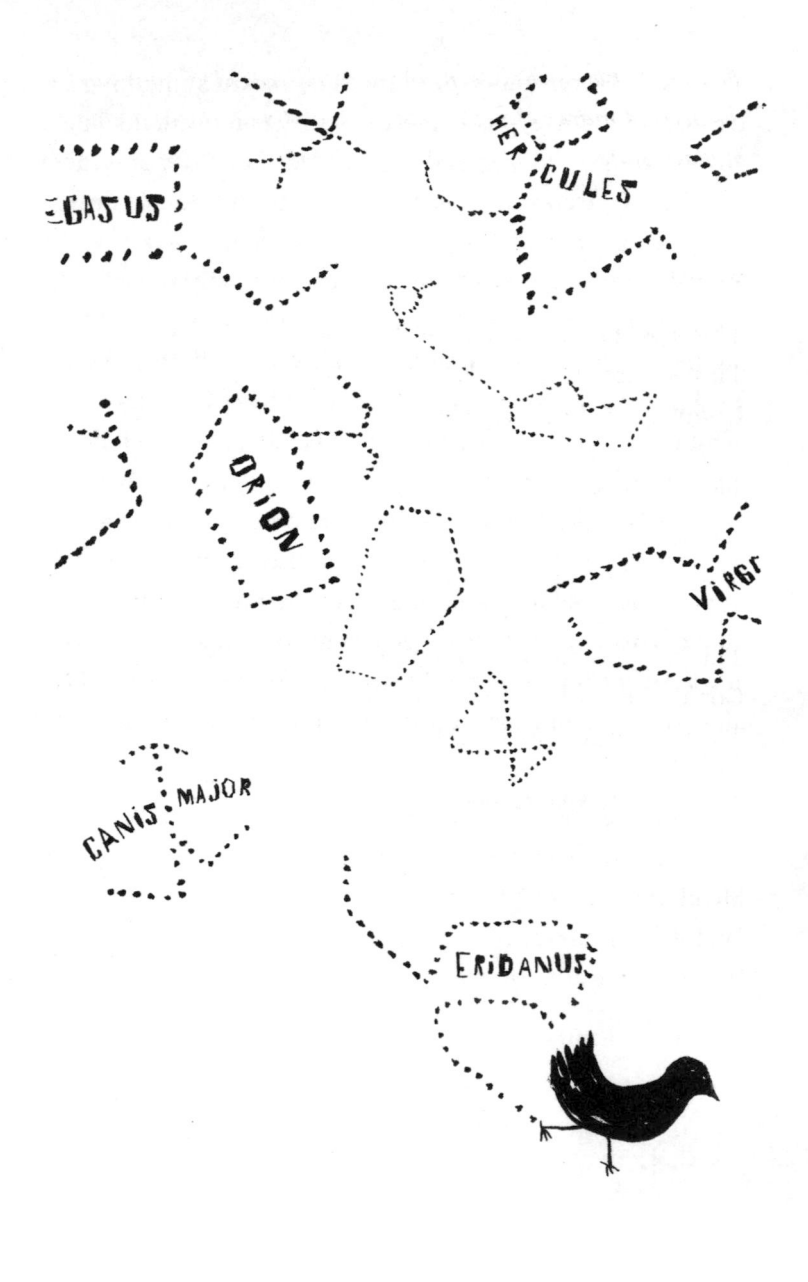

The snow, two inches deep, is beginning to slowly thaw and the myriad marks of birds' feet show up like a constellation of black stars.

✳

BC:AD

This was the moment when Before
Turned into After, and the future's
Uninvented timekeepers presented arms.

This was the moment when nothing
Happened. Only dull peace
Sprawled boringly over the earth.

This was the moment when even energetic Romans
Could find nothing better to do
Than counting heads in remote provinces.

And this was the moment
When a few farm workers and three
Members of an obscure Persian sect
Walked haphazard by starlight straight
Into the kingdom of heaven.

U. A. Fanthorpe

'There's little of the melancholy element in her, my lord:
she is never sad but when she sleeps, and not ever sad
then; for I have heard my daughter say, she hath often
dreamed of unhappiness and waked herself with
laughing.'

William Shakespeare, *Much Ado About Nothing*

✴

*Yesterday morning a rabbit, nibbling in the sun, cast a
shadow of its ears on the frost, which looked just like candlelight shadows thrown on the wall at children's bedtime.*

✴

' "I can't get through February without finding religion."
Items to help *Tatler* readers on their religious journey
including Jesus sandals (£120 from Yohji Yamamoto), a
sacred-heart skateboard (£30 from Benetton), a clutch of
votive candles, a light-up laughing Buddha, a rosary neck-
lace and a crucifix coatstand.'

From *The Tablet*, quoting *Tatler*

'Now there was a day when the sons of God came to present themselves before the Lord, and Satan came also among them.

'And the Lord said unto Satan, "Whence comest thou?" Then Satan answered the Lord, and said, "From going to and fro in the earth, and from walking up and down in it."'

Job 1:6–7

✳

'If she be furnish'd with a mind so rare
She is alone th' Arabian bird . . .'

William Shakespeare, *Cymbeline*

✳

Letter to the Daily Telegraph — *not sent*

Sir,
Look, let them get their act together, put it on the back burner, and, at the end of the day, kick-start it into the long grass. It must be abundantly clear at this moment in time we need a level playing field (if we are not to score own goals) free of clichés lobbed at us daily by politicians and experts who are encouraged to expose themselves in the media but not, thankfully, in the Full Monty.
Yours faithfully
A.G.

'But in the middle of the nineteenth century naturalists and physicists assured the world in the name of Science, that salvation and damnation are all nonsense, and that predestination is the central track of religion, inasmuch as human beings are produced by their environment, their sins and good deeds being only a series of chemical or mechanical reactions over which they have no control.'

G. B. Shaw, Introduction to *Heartbreak House*

✳

This morning the frost is in straight architectural patterns in the shade of the house and the grass is golden green in sunlight.

✳

'Thou gavest them a burning pillar of fire, both to be a guide of the unknown journey, and a harmless sun to entertain them honourably.'

Wisdom of Solomon 18:3

✳

'A pause just long enough for an angel to pass, flying slowly.'

Ronald Firbank, *Valmouth*

Postcard from John Quentin from Liverpool:

'After lunch, a visit to the Anglican Cathedral. In the entrance two signs: recommended by Egon Ronay – Ronay 1993–1994. Diners can be viewed behind glass, from the choir. A bazaar was taking place in the western half, back half, of the nave; the shop filled one of the transepts. There one could buy jams, jewellery, and a book called *Beyond the Final Whistle: A Life of Football and Faith*. When we left, a youth was about to abseil from the top of the Tower into the space between the transepts. An announcement told us his name was Tony.'

✻

'American lawyer in exchange with expert witness for the prosecution:
"Doctor," says the great lawyer, "before you performed the autopsy did you check for a pulse?"
"No."
"So then it's possible the patient was alive when you began the autopsy?"
"No."
"How can you be so sure?"
"Because his brain was sitting in a jar on my desk."
"Is it possible the patient could have been alive, none the less?"
"Well, it is possible that he could have been alive and practising law somewhere."'

 Trollopiana, no. 49 (John Letts)

' "Before Abraham was, I am," is the saying of Christ; yet is it true in some sense, if I say it of my self; for I was not onely before my self, but Adam, that is, in the Idea of God, and the decree of that Synod held from all Eternity. And in this sense, I say, the World was before the Creation, and at an end before it had a beginning; and thus was I dead before I was alive: though my grave be England, my dying place was Paradise: and Eve miscarried of me, before she conceiv'd of Cain.'

Sir Thomas Browne, *Religio Medici*

✳

'Any man's *death* diminishes *me*, because I am involved in *Mankind*; And therefore never send to know for whom the *bell* tolls; It tolls for *thee*.'

John Donne, 'Devotions'

✳

'But the multiplying brood of the ungodly shall not thrive, nor take deep rooting from bastard slips, nor lay any fast foundation.'

Wisdom of Solomon 4:3

Acknowledgements

The publishers wish to thank the following copyright holders for permission to quote copyrighted material:

'We and They', 'The Roman Centurion's Song' and 'My Boy Jack' by Rudyard Kipling. Reproduced by permission of A. P. Watt Ltd on behalf of the National Trust for Places of Historic Interest or Natural Beauty.

'Legend' from *Collected Poems 1951–2000* by Charles Causley, first published by Macmillan, 2000. Reproduced by permission of David Higham Associates.

'Brief Lives in not so Brief' by Ogden Nash from *Candy is Dandy: The Best of Ogden Nash*. First published in Great Britain in 1983 by André Deutsch Ltd under the title *I Wouldn't Have Missed it: Selected Poems of Ogden Nash*. Reprinted by permission of André Deutsch Ltd.

The Orion Publishing Group Ltd for permission to reprint extracts from 'The Bright Field', 'The Garden', 'A Thicket in Lleyn' and 'The Message' from *Collected Poems* by R. S. Thomas.

'Fairy Tale' from *Selected Poems* by Miroslav Holub, translated by Ian Milner and George Theiner (Penguin